Messages from Beyond

A Spiritual Guidebook

by

Michele Livingston

Messages from Beyond

Front cover image artwork by Todd Jumper.

FIRST SUNBURY PRESS EDITION
Printed in the United States of America
February 2011

ISBN 978-1-934597-31-6

Published by:
Sunbury Press
Lemoyne, PA

www.sunburypress.com

Lemoyne, Pennsylvania   USA

Acknowledgments

I wish to first thank all of my wonderful clients, who inspired me to write this guidebook. Your thought-provoking questions, asked at my seminars, in my Divine Wisdom columns and in consultation sessions compelled me to seek these spiritual answers.

Next, I acknowledge and thank my husband and soul partner, Jon Robert Stroh, for his patience and support during this project.

I thank Vicky Sgagias for her literary contributions that greatly enhanced the flow and clarity of these messages.

Finally, I acknowledge the Creator, my angels, guides and beloved departed who encourage and protect me on my path through life and provided me with the determination to complete this manuscript.

All souls were created in the beginning and are finding their way back to whence they came.

Edgar Cayce

Contents

Introduction

Welcome to the world of spirit—one of unconditional love and divine guidance. This guidebook is a compilation of information that I have shared with my clients over a twenty-year span at my seminars, group sessions and one-on-one consultations. The material covers a broad range of topics presented in a concise manner for easy reference.

Everyone has the ability to receive guidance, promptings and help from spiritual realms. Awareness is all it takes. I happen to be a direct channel that receives messages from the other side; I'm a liaison who bridges the gap between our physical, third-dimensional world and the spirit world of the fourth dimension. Children are easily aware of invisible realms between the ages of one and five. They may talk to unseen souls or angels and play with invisible playmates during those first few years of life. Therefore, to keep my abilities pure, I have tried to retain a childlike spirit within. I approach my work with an open mind and do not censor the information that is relayed to me.

Before I discovered my potential as a medium, my career was that of an artist. When I began advanced drawing and painting at the age of three, my mother felt encouraged to enroll me in art school. For four decades, my careers went from teaching art in public schools, to traveling the country showing and selling my artwork, to owning an art gallery that featured my collection of prints and paintings..

My true awareness of energy patterns around others started in my early forties. I first saw relevant symbols and initials around people that demanded my attention. As such, I began to offer psychic consultations, or readings. During one session, I was shocked to see a departed human soul standing next to my female client. It was the soul of her grandfather, and he telepathically gave me messages and information about their family. A few months later, angels and spirit guides appeared in readings, along with numerous departed relatives. The angels' and guides' energy patterns seemed higher and more advanced than the human souls of relatives or friends.

Today I'm an author, columnist, artist, counselor and psychic medium. I have also enjoyed hosting my own radio talk show and made numerous appearances on TV. I still enjoy creating visionary artwork, but most of all I see the rewards of helping others along their spiritual path to enlightenment. I hope that this guidebook will be instrumental in awakening your soul. The techniques, affirmations, thoughts, revelations and my personal experiences will offer you insight into your own life, ultimately providing you with a sense of balance, well-being and peace.

All my best and blessings,

Michele A. Livingston

Part I: Conscious Manifestation

To manifest what we want in life, we must first implement the following equation: guided thought plus the energy of intent equals results in tangible form. Only then will our *desires* come to fruition.

You have probably heard about positive thinking or guiding your thoughts. The reason these ideas have garnered momentum is grounded in the belief that thoughts are things. As human beings, we need to be mindful of our thinking patterns. Thoughts are electromagnetic energy impulses that travel through the universe. Consequently, we absolutely attract what we think!

Most of us have never been taught about the power of the mind, how to program it or our ability to manifest desires. To begin attracting what we want and need is as easy as making a grocery list. First, we think about what we want and write it down, which is "guided thought." Then, we drive to the market and buy the items, which puts into motion the "energy of intent." Lastly, we return home with our groceries and put them away, seeing that our desires and actions brought "results in tangible form." Thought plus energy equals form—
a process known as conscious manifestation.

The equation can be applied to finding a mate, creating a support team, pinpointing your soul purpose, attracting abundance and much more. Also, there is tremendous power in prayer, and when we pray over our "wish lists," it gives them positive, light-filled energy. In the chapters that follow, simple exercises that you can apply to your own life will be revealed. And trust me, the amazing results are bound to astonish you.

1 - *Attracting a Companion*

Meeting the perfect mate is the most rewarding experience. And yet, it can be an exhausting search. Are you tired of meeting the wrong partner? Or even settling for second best? Have you noticed a negative pattern of attracting the same type of personalities? You are not alone. Many people struggle with this dilemma. Don't give up hope. The good news is that attracting your perfect companion is much easier than you may think.

The fact is we are all children of God and deserve to have a perfect mate with whom we can share our lives. Most of us want a team player to be our equal, to be supportive as we experience life's hills and valleys. Some desire a homebody, while others look for an outdoorsy type. The possibilities are endless. However, it is crucial to *really* know yourself and what type of person would complement you best. Allow yourself the time to focus on the qualities and characteristics that are important to you, and be specific. Generalizing is counterproductive. Once you have solidified the details, write them down—all of them. Send your desire out into the universe to see them return in tangible results. Remember, thought plus energy equals form.

A great way to begin this process is by sitting down with a pen and a blank sheet of paper. Close your eyes, clear your mind and take several deep breaths. Write your full given name at the top of the paper. Next, write down the following affirmation:

Dear Lord, my heart is healed from past relationships. I am now breaking away from any and all negative patterns of attraction. I am now ready to attract my true soul mate, companion and husband (or wife) for our highest good. I want him (or her) to be eligible, willing to commit and in love with me.

Thereafter, list the qualities that you want in another human being. Try to fine-tune your descriptions and zero in on five of the most crucial qualities. Even though many of us are attracted to certain physical characteristics or financial security, it's the qualities of the person that we truly fall in love with. These may include someone who is appreciative, trustworthy, honest, fun-loving and so on. Really open your mind and dig deep into your heart to think about these things. This is, after all, the person you are choosing to spend the rest of your life with.

To complete your list for a significant other, write the following:

I am now ready to attract this person for both our highest good.

Make two copies of the completed paper. One should go into your purse, wallet or briefcase so that the energy and intent is with you throughout the day. The other copy should go on your nightstand or in your pillowcase while you sleep. Pray over the list once a week. Know and believe your perfect companion will be brought to you by the universal law of attraction.

In earthly time, it takes approximately two to twenty-four months to see results. I can attest to this, not only from my client's success stories, but my own. Two months after I made my list, I met my wonderful husband on Valentine's Day; he has every quality I wrote down, and handsome to boot!

2 - *Targeting Your Soul Purpose*

What's the purpose of my life? What's my mission? Finding answers to these loaded questions is not easy. But with a little help from this chapter, you'll know how to assert yourself and initiate the quest for betterment, personally and professionally. So if there's a void in your life or you're at a crossroads, rest assured that it's just a part of the journey!

Understanding our soul's purpose is instrumental to understanding ourselves. Our souls are always evolving and progressing. We learn lessons and retain knowledge from each earthly incarnation we experience. Before birth, our soul designates a specific virtue to be aware of or to learn through life. It could be patience, tolerance, humility or unconditional love, for example. If we are here to learn patience, then our patience will be tried and tested. The same can be said for tolerance, love or whatever other virtue is chosen. That is why every person is different and why some struggle with an issue that comes so easily to another. Each life has a recurring theme or pattern that emerges. This process acts as a catalyst to present opportunities for the soul to evolve.

To expedite our progress, we sometimes unconsciously choose jobs or careers that aid in mastering the virtue we were incarnated to learn. For example, it takes patience to serve as a nurse, teacher, counselor, psychologist or therapist. If self-discipline is the chosen virtue, serving in the military, becoming a nun or priest, or even being a professional athlete would fulfill that purpose. Such careers illustrate a soul that is serving humanity.

At the opposite end of the spectrum lies the other purpose that some souls incarnate to master—creativity. These individuals provide joy and enlightenment to others through creative means. Souls partaking in this endeavor seek outlets though music, art, writing and communication, to name a few. Their spark is guided by and encouraged through the Creator, who is within us and inspires these souls to share beauty with others through creative energy. These individuals are here to be independent and self-expressive. In summation, we are here to do one of two things–serve humanity or express ourselves through creativity.

Are you here to learn a virtue or purpose through a service position or by self-expressive means? You should love your career about 90 percent of the time. If you don't, you aren't doing what your soul came here to do. To better understand your soul's purpose, consider the following: if you are here to serve, you may work under a higher authority of churches, governments, corporations or administrations. Individuals that fall within this realm are often teachers, ministers, politicians, policemen or secretaries, to list a few. Mother Teresa is a great example of a soul who worked to serve humanity. We couldn't all walk the streets of Calcutta cleaning lepers' wounds, but she loved her work and was doing what her soul sent her here to do.

If your soul is here to express itself, you need a lifestyle that encourages independence. A defining characteristic of these individuals is their free spirit.. People who choose this mission are social creatures, and many excel as entrepreneurs. Some examples are fashion designers, journalists, architects, artists and, of course, anything to do with the arts, mainly music and theater.

Are you here to learn a virtue or purpose through a service position or by self-expressive means? Ask yourself this simple question: do I love what I do? We all have bad days, but if you find that 90 percent of the time you love what you do, be confident in your path and purpose. If not, and you feel lost or unhappy, reconsider your direction—no matter where you are or what you're doing.

Before making any decisions, search your soul and capture your personal essence. Focus. Think about what you are naturally gifted at, what brings you fulfillment and what you once dreamed of becoming. Clear your mind and really allow yourself the opportunity to answer honestly. Don't allow thoughts of stability, financial security or other people influence your answers or interrupt your motivation. Apply the following exercise and affirmation once you've given this adequate consideration and have a solid understanding of self.

On a blank sheet of paper write your full given name at the top and then this:

I call upon my divine guides, angels and the Creator to show me my soul's true purpose, the virtue I need to be aware of and my true mission for this lifetime.

Fold the paper in half vertically. On the left side list several things you love to do and see how those things correlate with your current life and career. On the right side, make a list of the things you're good at doing—skills, talents, good qualities and successes. Herein lies the key to why you are here and your soul purpose. When you do the work you love and are meant to do, you also learn or become aware of the virtues you need to master. Digest the information and complete the process by asking for help. Say a prayer to the Creator for opportunities that will incorporate the items on your list. You may start to realize things that you hadn't been privy to before, which will now suddenly direct you to a new place. Answers and options will begin to present themselves, and the perfect vocation will ultimately be revealed.

3 - Magnetizing Abundance

The Bible states we are here "to have life and have it more abundantly." The more we have in all areas of our lives, the more we can share with others. I have seen many people hesitate to ask for things because they don't feel worthy. Some feel guilty, and others just don't realize the power of affirmation. Don't allow yourself to entertain any of those reasons or be deterred from experiencing the joy of the things you want. Ask the universe to give you what you desire, and wait to receive it. At the beginning of each week, say the following:

This week I am experiencing a miracle regarding abundance.

Each word in the above-referenced affirmation plays a pivotal role in establishing the power of it. "This week" puts a time parameter on the phrase. "I am" is a direct statement to the universe. "Experiencing a miracle" means that miracles can come from many places or sources. "Regarding abundance" targets all good things.

Open your mind to the meaning of abundance. It could come to you in the form of gifts—people buying or giving you things. It may present itself as an opportunity at work. It might literally mean finding money on the street, winning a contest or even getting an unexpected discount at the register. While you might have a specific idea of what you want, it's best to keep an open mind at the beginning of each week. Witness how the universe works to deliver you the things that will benefit your life the most.

After receiving any form of miracle abundance, remember to say, "Thanks. I deserve it!" You are sending a message to the universe that you are worthy. A couple of years ago, I received an e-mail from one of my clients who had experienced a huge miracle of abundance. Brenda said the following:

"I really didn't believe in praying for money or abundance in my life because personally I never felt worthy to receive. Then my dog became seriously ill and I didn't even have enough money for the vet. At my wits end, I got down on my knees and said the miracle abundance affirmation with urgency. The next few days were nothing short of miraculous. The vet actually called me and told me to bring my beloved pet in for treatment. They would give me free medical assistance.

"Then two days later my mother was in a market and on a whim bought a scratch-off lottery ticket, something she had never done before. She instantly won $1 million in the Pennsylvania lottery! My mother gifted me with a new home and paid off all of my debts. It was interesting because I was receiving disability pensions and benefits. If I had won the money, I would have had to relinquish all of it. Now I truly believe in the abundance of the universe. After witnessing it for myself, I boldly stated, 'Thanks. I deserve it,' and meant it. Ever since, I say the miracle abundance phrase every week and my life continues to improve."

Here is another powerful daily affirmation to say:

Money comes easily and frequently.

Say this throughout the day and evening. Again, the universe is simple and at your command. When that thought is consistently sent out, you will see your financial situation change for the better.

4 - Protecting Yourself from Negativity

Our physical bodies shelter our souls, and around our bodies—extending approximately five feet in diameter—is the human aura. The aura, or etheric body, is an electromagnetic field that has been photographed with Kirlian photography. Every living, breathing entity— plants, animals and humans—has an aura. This aura of light can expand when we are happy and in good health. Similarly, when we're ill, depressed or sad, the aura shrinks. The smaller the aura is, the more vulnerable we become to the negative energy around us. In fact, we become like living sponges and unknowingly absorb the dramas, pain and problems of others. An example of this is going to work feeling great but returning home exhausted, depleted, irritable, frustrated, anxious or depressed after listening to a myriad of problems from co-workers all day.

Protection against negativity is of utmost importance, as our physical, spiritual and mental well-being depends upon it. There are two ways to keep your aura in check. The first way involves the actual cleansing of the auric field. The aura can be cleansed with smoke, crystals or even feathers, but the most effective way is through water. Of the four elements—water, earth, air and fire—water is the most healing, purifying and therapeutic. Soaking baths are excellent for auric cleansing, especially when you add Epsom salts and baking soda. (Refer to "Cleansing the Aura" in Part II.) Drinking eight glasses of steam-distilled or purified water each day will also aid in cleansing internal organs. And here's a fun fact: squeezing some real lemon juice, which is alkaline, in your glass of drinking water will help to balance your system.

The second method of protection is prayer. The prayer of protection is a potent weapon against attacks of negativity. When you wake up in the morning, go to a mirror and visualize a bubble of pure white light surrounding your body. Say the following:

> *Dear Lord, protect me this day. Protect me physically, emotionally and mentally. Protect my aura and my soul. Let me only attract people into my space today for my highest good and theirs; and let me only attract opportunities and situations into my space for my highest good and the highest good of humanity.*

By incorporating the prayer into your daily life, you are actively engaging in positive energy and stopping the nuisance of negativity. You'll notice the drainers, pullers, takers and dumpers fading. Friends who distance themselves or whom you no longer feel close to are people who negatively affected your spirit. They were toxic to your aura and weren't contributing to your highest good. Before long, new friends and social circles will form, and you will feel energized, excited and healthier.

5 - *Clearing Negative Energy from an Environment*

Negative energy in a home or office can be immensely taxing on productivity, health and tranquility. Homes inhabited by previous owners may be susceptible to the lingering energy of quarrels, arguments and hardships they once endured. Believe it or not, many homes also harbor the nature of death that their owners met, some who died tragically, unexpectedly or after a long battle with disease. Unrest may also be present when a home or office is built on an Indian burial ground or near a Civil War battlefield, for example. While it may be unnerving to consider the history of your home, office or property, it should be done, especially when it lacks the harmonious energy that it should exude.

In situations where negative energy is determined, the environment may experience restlessness, energy drain and a dark, foreboding feeling. Some discarnate spirits are earthbound because they do not realize they have died in a traumatic way, while others refuse to go to the light. Many souls want to stay on the earth plane to oversee their earthly possessions or property. However, it's not always the spirits of the departed that influence the tone of a home. Sometimes troubled people leave their emotional baggage behind when they move on, and when you move into their space, you imbibe their emotional energy patterns and inherit the negativity.

Before you move into a new environment (like an older home), follow some preliminary instructions to cleanse the territory. Begin by opening all the doors and windows to let fresh air flow through. For deceased souls that are still clinging on to your new space, demand that they go to "the light." Avoid being fearful when you make this command. Many discarnate spirits feed off fear, and your confidence may be the booster they need.

Once the cleansing has been completed, purification follows. There are three ways to go about purifying, so consider the following methods and what would be best-suited for you and your unique situation.

Smudging your home with Native American sweet grass or sage sticks is the first option. To do this, take a bowl and light the stick over it. Blow out the flame and fan the smoke around your body. Use the bowl to catch the ashes. Start in the basement and go room to room (including closets) and hold the lit smudge stick up to each of the four corners of every room. Each time say the following invocation:

> *This home is cleansed in the pure white light of God's goodness and protection. It is a safe and blessed haven in which to live. Cleansing power of the sage (or sweet grass), drive away all that is negative. All*

*who dwell here live in peace, love and joy. Anything
not of the light, leave now!*

When completed, smother the end of the smudge stick
in your bowl or hold it under running water. Be absolutely
certain that your stick is extinguished! Wrap it in a plastic
bag and store it for future use.

An alternative to the smudge stick is spraying holy
water. This method is just as effective in protecting your
environment and will rid it of unwanted energy. If you can't
obtain holy water, put a clear glass jar filled with steam-
distilled water on a windowsill in direct sunlight for three
days. Put the water into an atomizer. While you're alone,
spray the holy water in each room and say out loud:

*Anything that is not of the light, leave now. You're
not welcome here!*

After following those instructions, spray some water on
your fingers and make the sign of the cross at the top of
each doorway (standing securely on a stool if you need to).
Be prepared to get chills; you might immediately feel the
energy lift.

If you're uncomfortable with the smudge stick or holy
water, this next option may be the best avenue for you to
pursue. The "white lighting" technique is less complicated
but still viable and works just the same to eradicate
negative energy. Before going to sleep, visualize (in your
mind's eye) a very large, pure white sheet of light. Place
this sheet of light under the foundation of your home or
office. Slowly visualize the white sheet rising up through
the basement, the first floor, the second floor and so on. As
the sheet moves, allow the negative energy to be collected
onto the sheet and visualize it as gray matter. This will
accumulate the negative energy of discarnate spirits or
living individuals who recently inhabited the space. It will
also aid in releasing your own negative thoughts or moods.

Continue to move the sheet of light up through the
entire building until it reaches the roof. Raise it to six feet

above the roofline. You will now notice even more dark gray patches that have accumulated there. Now slowly take the four corners of the white sheet and fold them together, making a bundle with the dark matter collected inside. In your mind's eye, tie a big knot on the top with a gold ribbon and send it way out into space! Watch as it disappears. Your home will be cleansed and you'll experience a new calm, peace and contentment.

These techniques are also helpful when you are trying to sell your home. If you have lived in an environment for an extended period of time, memories and emotions are bound to the physical property. As a result, you may be unconsciously clinging to the space, and the home won't sell. If this is the case, the white lighting technique can expedite the release of any attachments you have.

6 - *Bringing Angelic Energy into the Home*

If you have cleared your environment by using the techniques from the previous chapter, now is the time to invite angels into your home. Before beginning this process, it's important to understand what angels are and why they exist.

Angels are "light beings" created by God. They assist human souls on the journey through eternity. They have never inhabited a human body, but they have materialized into the human form during times of need. Angels are in a very high-energy frequency. There are twelve dimensions of light and energy. These dimensions are not linear, but overlapping. We live on the earth plane, the third dimension. The angelic kingdom is on the eleventh dimension.

I have been blessed with the ability to see angels. Today, many people seek me out so that they too can get in touch with their angels through me. When I see an angel, it looks like a large, shimmering column of light, and then it starts to project "essence features" that are either male or female. Although they are androgynous, or sexless, beings, the essence features help to personalize them for the person I'm reading. Every human has a guardian or companion angel that never leaves their side, and this is the angel that usually appears in a reading. I also work with three of the archangels: Archangel Michael, who is the divine angel of protection; Gabriel, who is the divine messenger of truth; and the divine healer, Raphael.

Although angels do not have total free will (they were created to serve humankind), we can invoke them into our living environment. One way is by burning white, pink or pale blue pillar candles or votives. White is the color of purity and the higher spiritual dimensions; pink is the color of unconditional love; blue represents calm and peace. Angels are also attracted to water because of the purifying and healing properties it possesses. Cultivate an angelic presence in your home by incorporating water elements into your surroundings. Achieving water energy could be as simple as floating a flower in a crystal bowl or installing a tabletop fountain. In addition to soliciting the presence of angels, listening to running water can be very soothing to the senses—something we could all stand to benefit from. I also recommend live plants and fresh flowers for your home. Plants put oxygen into the air, cleanse the environment and magnetize angels.

Every home should dedicate an area to prayer and meditation, a private sanctuary that promotes wellness and spiritual light. Establishing a harmonious environment encourages angelic contact, and the altar you designate will prove to be instrumental. Start by covering a small table or shelf with a white cloth, and include the four elements—earth, air, fire and water. Earth may be represented with a small plant, gemstone or rock grouping. Water can be symbolized with a fountain or some holy water. Burning incense or defusing essential oils stimulates the flow of air, while candles denote the energy of fire. Arrange your candles in groups of three, representing the Holy Trinity—the balance of mind, body and spirit. Next, place images that inspire you by the candles, such as angels, Blessed Mother Mary (who is known as Queen of the Angels), Jesus, the saints, Quan

Yin, Buddha, Shiva or *your* departed loved ones. Place special objects on your altar that are blessed and important to you. You could perhaps use a cross, the Star of David, rosary beads, heirloom jewelry or whatever symbol you choose. The sacred place you create will be where your angels will gather; here you will feel their protection, loving presence, peace and guidance.

7 - Utilizing a Method to Reduce or Stop Smoking

One of the most revered spiritual traditions of Native American Indians was passing the peace pipe while sitting in a circle. This custom represented communion and unity to them. They grew their own tobacco and herbs, which were free of preservatives, chemicals and additives. While smoking poses several health risks, the organic tobacco that Native Americans used was very different from the tobacco we have come to know today. In fact, many Native Americans lived well into their late nineties or even past the century mark.

Unfortunately, tobacco now is controlled by an industry that relies on manufacturing products that seriously harm the people who use it. Scientists have found twenty-three major toxins in cigarettes, many of them sprayed on the tobacco as it is grown. One such product is formaldehyde, a preservative. Another is a strong chemically addictive drug that increases dependence. Although it is difficult to quit smoking, it's not impossible. Hypnotherapy and nicotine patches have helped some people, and others have succeeded with the drug Wellbutrin.

When an individual is a heavy smoker, the poisons stay in the air and cling to their auric field—the electromagnetic energy field surrounding the body. I can immediately determine whether someone smokes or not by one look at them. I can see the gray look around their face and in their aura. In order to continue on the spiritual journey and advance our souls, purification is crucial. Smoking is detrimental to our bodies, souls and purposes and must be stopped. My guides have given me a method that aids in quitting smoking. This approach succeeds because it works by gradually weaning the body and mind off of the chemicals instead of abruptly shocking the system.

If you smoke a pack a day, start the first week by taking one cigarette out of the pack each day. Break that cigarette in half and throw it away. Immediately you are reducing your intake by seven cigarettes a week. This also makes you aware of when you smoke and how much you smoke, and it helps to instill self-discipline. The second week take out two cigarettes per pack, the third week three per pack and so on.

Don't give up and keep up with the technique! Even reducing your smoking by one cigarette per pack is better than none. By the twentieth to twenty-fifth week, you will have literally weaned yourself off these deadly weeds and the chemically addictive drugs they contain. Should you relapse down the road, begin this process immediately to achieve smoking cessation as soon as possible.

8 - Using the "I Am" Technique

As we have learned, thoughts are energy impulses that travel out into the cosmos and return to us. Just like a computer, we get back what we program in. We are the product of our thinking. As such, programming what we say influences our beliefs, and in turn, our lives. I have found that a simple exercise contributes to this practice. By simply stating the phrase "I am" and following it with an adjective serves to validate the phrase by proving it. "I am" sayings are powerful because we are reaffirming to the universe that we already have what we need—it already exists. "I am smart.." "I am beautiful." "I am successful." The truth is we are all the things we need, but sending it out into the universe allows the thought to be acknowledged and gives us the momentum to believe it. Positive statements beginning with "I am" open the door to the divine energy that dwells within us.

In the biblical sense, God is referred to as the great "I Am." When Moses went up to Mount Sinai and received the

Ten Commandments, he asked the voice behind the burning bush, "Who shall I say sent me?" The voice replied, "Tell them '*I Am*, that *I Am* sent you.'" The name God gave to Moses was *I Am*. We are co-creators with God, and when we use "I am" affirmations, they become empowered. When we participate in this exercise, we release the full activity of God into our lives.

Before saying these positive statements, clear your mind and take a few deep breaths. The "I am" affirmations can be said and reinforced in any quiet meditative place. Do this while walking in nature, soaking in the bathtub or before going to sleep at night. Personalize your list to suit your needs. An example of your list can include:

I am healed from the crown of my head to the soles of my feet... I am important... I am thinking important thoughts... I am compassionate... I am assertive... I am confident... I am loving myself and others unconditionally... I am joyful... I am debt free... I am intuitive... I am attracting good people into my life... I am gaining recognition... I am blessed... and whatever else you feel compelled to say.

When we say these affirmations, we are saying, "I am already there!" This expedites the action of the "I am" affirmations and puts everything in the present. Say these positive personal statements daily—your life will change for the better.

9 - *Releasing Departed Loved Ones*

Our souls incarnate in groups that are predetermined before birth. Everyone we know, whether intimately or just in passing, is a soul connected to us. Some of these bonds are stronger than others, but every soul we come across serves a purpose, regardless of relationship status. The more we understand about ourselves, the more we can make sense of these bonds.

We enter soul agreements within these groups before incarnating. An example would be to offer help and support each other, like that of husband and wife. It could also mean to work things out karmicly or rectify what may have transpired in a past life. Family relationships are another example of soul agreements. We agree on who will be our children, parents, spouses and so on. Our bonds supersede coincidence; we elect to be a part of a group long before we meet on the earth plane. As such, when someone we dearly love passes away, it's devastating for those left behind on earth.

We must remember and take comfort in the truth about death: the physical body may be gone, but the soul is very much alive. The soul retains its mind, personality and memory bank. And soul progression continues to flourish on the other side before and after life on the earth plane. For example, furthering our spiritual studies at temples of wisdom and learning can take place. Child prodigies such as Mozart, who composed music at an early age, probably honed the gift of composition before incarnating. Souls can train to be guides of those still on the earth plane, and even help other souls cross over. We can join in with other souls to help influence world peace or work on other issues such as global starvation, natural disasters or health epidemics.

Since there is no time in the next dimension, we might choose to relax for a while. Some souls pursue this by creating beauty with their minds—designing gardens, waterfalls and beautiful landscape environments. We can still our minds, meditate if we wish or study with ascended masters. When an individual experiences a lingering, painful passing over (as in a cancer situation), there is a form of cocooning that sometimes happens after transition to ease and relax the soul.. The physical, mental and emotional states are often exhausted during the transition, and the soul needs to regroup and adjust to the higher, faster frequency of the fourth dimension. Regardless of the specifics, every soul passes because it has chosen to exit the earth plane; the soul lessons were accomplished for that lifetime.

As we have our own pursuits here on the earth plane, souls on the other side also have their own agendas. The greatest thing to do for the departed is to release them so that they can be at peace and get on with their progression. When we unreasonably cling to those who have passed on by mourning obsessively or begging for their return, they cannot rest. We must understand, encourage and allow them to be engaged in whatever they have chosen to do on the other side without interrupting the process with our excessive grief. Give departed souls the freedom to rest in their cocoon state; they may desperately need it after passing. While the pain we feel when someone dies may be unbearable at times, we must be stronger than our emotions. Our inability to cope with death can wreck havoc on a soul trying to adjust to the new frequency, and we should make a conscious effort to accept death and move forward in our own lives.

Always remember the departed and the beautiful memories you share, but relinquish the grip that binds you to them. The following chapter's information will help you look at your loss from a new perspective and let you look at situations from another viewpoint. Always remember—your happiness is their happiness, so get on with your life ...for life is for the living!

10 - *Helping Relatives and Friends to Cross Over*

Every human soul chooses to enter the earth plane to love unconditionally and learn soul lessons. The soul chooses its parents, date of birth and time to pass on. When the soul is in the body, we have certain trials we must work through. That is the human condition. A person knows "soulwise" when it is their time to go but may consciously cling to the human body for a number of reasons.

I have friends who are hospice workers, and they have explained that sometimes a person needs verbal "permission to let go." I have also witnessed this phenomenon firsthand. My stepfather lingered with cancer, but his soul refused to release from his body. He was concerned about his bookstore along with his collection of antiques and collectibles. Although he was not materialistic, this sentimental accumulation represented a lifetime of collecting. Similarly, my stepsister lay in pain for months with breast cancer. She did not want to leave her beautiful champion show dogs behind even though she was so tired and longed to go. My dear mother also lingered, admitting she wanted to see me married before she made the transition.

In all these cases, the person longed for heaven but felt a physical pressure to cling to their body. That's not always the case, though. Sometimes a person will linger simply out of fear of the unknown. There is a technique I used for all of my loved ones to facilitate and expedite their peaceful passing. If you need to be a facilitator for your loved ones to cross over, then I suggest the following exercise:

In your mind's eye, visualize the person you want to help to cross over and take their hand. Visualize a long tunnel in front of you. Let your soul gently start to walk their soul down the tunnel and you will see a pinpoint of light at the end. As you walk, call them by name and tell them that they had a good life and it's OK to let go, that they're going to a better place filled with love and light. Tell them they will reunite with their pets, friends and loved ones on the other side, will be greeted by angels and will be safe in God's keeping. Softly advise them to go in peace toward the light. Ahead, you will see the pinpoint of light become larger and brighter. You may even see departed loved ones waiting there yourself. When you have reached the end of the tunnel, let go of their hand and float backwards. You will see your loved one's silhouette in the light growing smaller and smaller. Then take a couple of deep breaths, and your soul will return to your own body.

Do this technique for a day or two. Your loved one's soul usually releases within twenty-four to forty-eight hours. This is a powerful service of love you are providing for them, and it should only be directed at those who are lingering and wish to depart.

Before departing, my mother's hospice nurse tried the same type of method on her. At the time, my mother had a very nosy roommate named Peep. The curtain was drawn between them, and the hospice worker stayed with my mother for about an hour, gently talking to her out loud. "You've lived a good life, and it's time to release. Let go. Go in peace. Go to the light," she reassured, urging my mother. The next day, the nurse entered my mother's room to see if she had passed overnight. To her utter surprise, Peep was the one to go. She had been listening to the nurse! Peep's soul was ready to let go; she just needed a nudge. With that said, you can never force someone's soul out of their body; it will only leave when it is ready. I feel that it is sometimes better to help the person in your mind's eye rather than physically tell them, but this can depend on the individual you are helping. I continued the technique with my mother and she passed peacefully the next morning.

11 - Balancing Energy with Gold and Silver Jewelry

What we wear—certain materials, a favorite color, jewelry with a particular gemstone or precious metal—affects our auric field. For example, wearing jewel-toned chakra colors from the heart region up to the top of the head expands the aura and raises the energy field. Emerald green, aqua, royal blue, purple and white all have the power to positively affect the aura. Likewise, a natural material such as silk is advantageous to wear because it enables energy to transmute. I know a well-known healer who wears nothing but silk, which is cool in the summer and warm in the winter. She claims wearing silk clothing helps her to balance not only her own energy field but also the auric field of others. The gemstone amethyst promotes healing when worn as jewelry (purple being the highest spiritual color) and rose quartz has properties to attract love (rose pink being the color of unconditional love).

The composition of gold and silver metal also emanates a certain energy that travels into the auric field. The precious metal gold was consistently worn in ancient Egypt. Gold was symbolic of the daytime and the sun, which was considered to emanate a masculine energy, also called yang. Gold also represented the solar cycles and Egypt's sun god, named Ra. They believed gold gave strength, enlightenment and power to the wearer. Gold protects us from negativity and helps with logic and left-brain situations. Silver, on the other hand, is a soft, mutable precious metal. Silver represents nighttime, the lunar cycle and moon, the goddess energy, mystical secrets of insight and the divine feminine (called yin). It also governs the right side of the brain, which deals with intuition.

Each individual on the earth plane has both a masculine and feminine side to his or her nature. The masculine side is physically strong, independent, assertive, analytical and competitive. The feminine side is soft, creative, emotional, nurturing and intuitive. The two polarities of masculine and feminine should be balanced and in harmony.

Make a conscious effort to alternate the wearing of gold and silver jewelry to reap the benefits of both. You might consider wearing gold jewelry the first half of a week then silver over the weekend or vice versa. Another way to balance yourself is to change your metals every other day. If you don't like jewelry, don't wear it. This advice is for people that love jewelry or consistently wear either gold or silver. You can also mix pieces of gold and silver and wear them at the same time.

By following this guidance, you'll have a new awareness that you imbibe what you wear into your aura. And with this knowledge, you will feel more centered, grounded and in harmony with yourself.

12 - Desiring Weight Loss

Obesity is an excess of body fat, and anyone who is about 20 percent over their ideal weight could be considered obese.

Life can be stressful. People overeat for a number of reasons, some of which are not totally related to habitual overeating (like hypothyroidism, glandular problems and diabetes). Boredom, emotional tension and a simple love of food are common reasons for overeating. It is also evident that people who have been sexually abused as children will unconsciously put on weight to "pad" themselves against feeling vulnerable. They may subconsciously think, "If I am not attractive, I won't be molested." A poor diet and lack of exercise may lead to being overweight. Some people retain water as well, so a simple herbal diuretic may be of value.

Permanent weight loss requires a commitment to being aware of your eating habits. In other words, chew your food thoroughly; eat slowly; try not to consume everything on your plate, etc. Regular exercise programs along with good elimination are also helpful. There is no easy fix, yet conscious manifestation can help. Say the following positive affirmation daily:

> *I am now happy and grateful for being at my ideal weight of ____. I am only eating foods and drinking beverages that are for my highest good. I am now monitoring my consumption of sugar, fats and carbohydrates. I am in perfect health. I am happy and grateful for looking thin and toned. I love and appreciate my body. I am disciplined with an exercise program. I am walking tall with excellent posture. I am happy for my recent weight loss.*

Putting your statements in the present expedites weight loss. This affirmation can be said several times a day until it enters the subconscious mind, and the universe will always bring you what you think and believe.

In addition, hypnotherapy can be a helpful tool to assist in weight loss. Most of us have eating habits that were acquired in early childhood. How many of us have heard "Eat everything on your plate; there are children starving in China" along with other things that are embedded deep in our subconscious minds? With hypnotherapy, you are able to identify and alter these misconceptions and help change lifelong eating habits.

Part II: Advancement of the Spiritual Journey

Our souls were created when God conceived us in His mind. Our Creator is like an eternal flame of wisdom and light, and our souls are sparks of that flame. God is an infinite source of intelligence and pure unconditional love. As His creation and with His blessing, we choose to incarnate into a human body time and again, to learn or become aware of certain soul lessons.

Every person embarks on a special mission to serve a specific purpose. As co-creators with God, we choose everything (like making soul agreements with other souls and deciphering specific virtues to master) before birth. Souls form groups and incarnate with certain parents, siblings, children, spouses and social circles. Environments and situations that contribute to and cultivate the learning experience are predetermined before entering the earth plane.

Various encounters and unique circumstances in life play an integral role in further developing our relationship with God. For example, if we incarnate to learn patience, we may choose a physical or mental disability so that waiting and awareness of patience are instilled. Or, a soul agreement to teach parents spiritual faith may entail a child passing away at an early age. Regardless of what hardships we endure, the ultimate plan is evolving our souls to become closer to the Creator. The grief and overwhelming losses we sometimes encounter propel us to search for clarity through the chaos, and that is where we find God.

Since the Lord surrounds us and is within us, every thought, motivation, action or experience that we have gives the Creator the opportunity to also experience His divine self through us. God knows us intimately, intensely feels our emotions, listens to our innermost thoughts and shares in our life experiences and decisions.

The human soul was conceived long before the physical form embodied it. Before entering the earth plane, souls floated freely through dimensions and created reality through their own thought forms. God then gifted the souls with a body as a way to greater express Himself. Along with the body and life came another precious gift—free will. All this introduced numerous complexities to the soul, because being alive meant the soul could experience physical sensations, partake in self-empowerment, make decisions and procreate.

As I've mentioned before, souls are on an evolutionary journey through eternity. The body is like a car that the soul uses to drive around in each lifetime. When the car (or body) is old and rusty, we junk it, go back to the fourth dimension, regroup and decide when to get a new one. When an individual soul feels it has evolved to the point of pure unconditional love and light, it stays in the other dimensions and does not reincarnate. Once the soul has evolved and reached "ascended master" status, it stays in the other realms to mentor and teach other souls about the life journey. This evolved state of being is likened to the Christ Consciousness—a compassionate state of total oneness with God. Enlightened souls form groups as master teachers and guide others on achieving soul progression.

The following chapters serve as a guide to bring you closer to the divine spark within. The information will enlighten you, help you to progress more rapidly as a human soul and ultimately give you the opportunity to advance in spiritual awareness.

1 - Cleansing the Aura

The aura is an electromagnetic energy field that surrounds the physical body and extends approximately three to five feet outside of it. It is where all that you are— your essence—is imprinted. Auras are not limited to humans. Every living being possesses one—plants, animals and even insects have auras.

In an attempt to capture the auric field on film, the Russians began photographing them in the 1950s. Using a special Kirlian camera, they found that when a leaf was cut from a plant, the aura of the leaf remained in place for a few minutes. Another stunning image revealed the aura of a missing leg from a man who had had it amputated during surgery. The photographs were proof that the auric field was conscious and alive. These special cameras capture the colors of auras that are normally invisible to the naked eye. Certain healers, massage therapists and medical intuitives can see these colors and shapes around individuals they work with. Some people have an innate ability to see auras, while others hone in on the skill by taking specialized courses.

Since the human aura is an extension of the soul and body, it holds a record of our thoughts, emotions and experiences. Thought patterns affect the light and vitality of an aura, so it is crucial to remain positive, loving and forgiving. Unfortunately, our own energy isn't the only factor that the aura encapsulates; it can also be influenced by the energy of others. Depression, illness and negativity can sometimes result from a contaminated aura, whether our own thoughts and life are contributing causes or someone around us is responsible.

To maintain and protect a healthy aura, it is imperative to cleanse it daily. In the morning, go to a full-length mirror and visualize an oval of pure white light surrounding your body. Say the following affirmation:

I am protected this day in the light and love of God and in all areas of my life. I am protected physically, emotionally, mentally and spiritually, along with my aura and soul.

At least once a week, take a warm soaking bath. A mineral spa can be created by using two cups of Epsom salts, two cups of baking soda and a few drops of lavender or rose oil. Add all of the ingredients to a warm, water-filled tub to benefit fully from the soothing effects they promise. Excluding your head, submerge your body into the water and allow the salts to relax your joints and muscles. This process will aid in expelling toxins from your body through the pores of your skin. The baking soda will draw out negativity while cleansing the auric field.

Soaking baths provide an ideal time to incorporate prayer and meditation into your life. Deep, restful sleep is another benefit to soaking. You'll feel refreshed and well-rested the following day. Consider burning white candles to attract radiant angelic beings into the room while you decompress in the water.

Another method of expanding and protecting the aura is adding certain colors to your wardrobe. Jewel-toned chakra colors vibrate from the heart region up to the top of the head. Examples of these colors are emerald green, teal, aqua, royal blue, purple and white; they all maximize the expansion and protection of the auric field. On the other hand, black, brown, navy and gray shrink the aura. Studies have shown that constantly wearing dark colors may actually cause illness.

Lastly, be good to yourself. A healthy diet in conjunction with drinking lots of purified water daily greatly benefits our bodies, souls and auras. Make and take the time to pray and meditate every day; try incorporating meditation during your soaking bath, and dedicate a peaceful hour before going to sleep to pray. Moderate or relinquish harmful chemicals like alcohol, nicotine, recreational drugs, sugar and caffeine. Take walks in nature and breathe in fresh, clean air, whether it is near the ocean, in the forest, in the mountains or in your own neighborhood. Exercise with stretching techniques such as yoga and Pilates. Get therapeutic massages once a month to help alleviate stress and release tension. And finally, have an attitude of gratitude, and count your blessings every single day.

Remember, awareness of these spiritual concepts is key. By using the aforementioned techniques, you will have a stronger, healthier and better-protected aura.

2 - The Exercise of Forgiveness

No ifs, ands or buts about it—forgiving someone who wronged us is one of the hardest things to do. Yet, it can be one of the most liberating. Believe it or not, forgiveness is synonymous with unconditional love. And partaking in the act of forgiveness relinquishes negative cords that, through Karma, can bind us to one another. Many of us unconsciously harbor feelings of anger and resentment toward others who have done us wrong, and it restricts our evolutionary soul journey.

Fortunately, through an effective exercise, you can conquer the bad feelings and release the toxicity they produce. Don't worry. There is no need to physically confront the people who have lied to you or abused, hurt or betrayed you. This exercise is done mind-to-mind and soul-to-soul. Depending on the severity of your situation(s), it can take up to three weeks to complete.

To begin, dedicate three nights a week to meditate, and commit to those specified days. Before you go to sleep the first night, go back in your mind to your early childhood years, ages one to five—the most developmentally impactful years of life. During those years you loved unconditionally, saw the world through the eyes of wonder and were sensitive, trusting, creative and imaginative. The first five years of life are when children are able to tap into the invisible realms and communicate with angels and departed loved ones. Unfortunately, it's also a time when a simple abuse that has been inflicted—whether it's verbal, mental or physical—can become lodged in the unconscious mind.

Think of those who may have hurt, abused, slighted, criticized or ignored you. One by one, visualize the person's face as plainly as you can, and surround it with pure white light. Say the following:

I know you are a hurting human being, and I don't like what you did to me. But you are still a child of God, and therefore I forgive you. I love you. I release you to the universe.

On the next scheduled night, do the same exercise for the elementary school years—ages six to twelve. You may recollect memories of teachers who were mean, abusive parents and neighbors, kids that teased you and so on. Visualize each person's face in your mind's eye, and surround their face with the white light of forgiveness. Repeat the affirmation. On a consecutive night, go into your teenage years—thirteen through nineteen. Continue the exercise for each decade of your life, through your twenties, thirties, forties and so on, until you reach your present age.

In the end you'll be a freer, happier and more peaceful person. This exercise will help you progress along your spiritual path. After the process, you will feel lighter. You may even lose weight and stop addictive behaviors. But most importantly, you are cutting karmic cords with these people so that you don't need to come back with them in another life to get it right.

If you find it difficult to do this exercise or feel that you may be missing individuals that have caused you pain, consider a facilitated version of this exercise called Kahuna Healing. It is often difficult to do healing work without a facilitator, and Kahuna Healing is a facilitated version of this procedure. *(Contact Michele Livingston or Jon Stroh for more information on Kahuna Healing.)*

Forgiveness is one of the highest forms of unconditional love. Christ set an example for us as he was being nailed to the cross when he said, "Forgive them for they know not what they do." Always remember the powerful message of those words, especially if you are having a hard time pursuing or completing this exercise.

3 - *The Power of Prayer and Meditation*

God—that is, the source of all—created souls eons ago. It should be Him whom we look to for support, guidance, love and light. One way to communicate with God is through prayer. When we pray, a positive energy pulse emanates from our hearts and minds to Him. Prayer enables us to unite with God more personally. We become empowered through this energy and should seek to do it daily. Rest assured that no prayer goes unheard or unanswered.

There is much to be said about the healing power of prayer. This common concept has garnered monumental attention because it works. Scientific studies have yielded miraculous results where the healing power of prayer positively affected plants, animals and humans. Healing prayers also help others to thrive in greater ways, so don't limit prayers to you and what is going on in your life. Pray for others and even for those who have passed away.

We release intense emotion and send compassionate love back into the universe through prayer. What we pray for comes back to us. Remember the laws of attraction? If we ask for another's healing, we may ourselves receive a healing. Plus, there is nothing complicated about praying. Keep it simple. Pray in a quiet place where you can't be distracted. Pray any time of the day or night. And always start off with an attitude of gratitude by counting your blessings. For example:

> *Dear Lord, thank you for my good health, my talents, my spouse, my children and my pets. Thank you for the new social circles and support groups you will send me in the future. Thank you for creating me and for letting me come to the earth plane to be productive and enrich other lives as I progress on my own spiritual journey.*

You'll feel better if you start your prayers by listing what you are thankful for. The next part of your prayer time should include your requests, which I call the "help me" part of praying:

With your will, help me to be more respectful, patient and humble. Help me to be focused and prioritize my time and energy. Give me greater clarity of my purpose and direction in life. With your will, help me to be more empathic and aware of others' feelings and needs. Give me a closer walk with you and help me to be more Christlike. Help the poor, the starving and the abused. Help our world to be at peace and protect us from harm...

And on it goes.

The third part is the "forgive me" list. In this part, you need to contemplate where you are *now* in your life, what you've done in the *past and* where you want to be in the *future.* This part of the prayer makes you aware of your own weaknesses and instills humility.

I recommend breaking down your prayers into those three parts; the structure will make it easier to be consistent on a daily basis. An answer will always come from praying, though it may not be in the time or way we expect. Pray daily and be open to the answers that come to you. Also, be relaxed and feel the soothing inner peace that results from praying.

I recommend doing with meditating what I suggested with praying: set aside (at least) three days a week for it. Meditating is great for balance and a wonderful tool for the mind-body-spirit connection. Meditation stills the mind, opens the senses, calms the spirit and helps us listen to our own higher soul knowledge. In addition, it brings us closer to our spirit guides, angels and the divine wisdom of God.

There are many ways to go about meditating. Some people partake in this ritual by closing their eyes and combining it with a relaxing soaking bath or while listening to calming music. Others enjoy meditating with their eyes open while walking alone in nature, enjoying the beauty of the changing seasons and listening to the wind or the rustling of the leaves. Regardless of your preference, this ritual lowers blood pressure, releases stress and puts you in touch with yourself. Through time, your inner voice will become clear and magnified and resonate peace throughout your mind, body and soul.

If you haven't tried meditating before or want to try a conventional method, I have some pointers. Sit in a straight-backed chair with your feet firmly planted on the floor. Close your eyes, take a few deep breaths and put your hands on your lap with your palms facing up. Visualize a thin cord of light coming out of your solar plexus (abdomen), your coccyx (tailbone) and both soles of your feet. These cords travel down to the center of the earth to anchor you. Next, think of a lovely and peaceful place and envision yourself there, like walking along the ocean, watching a vibrant sunset, meandering through a dense forest or sitting in a gazebo protected by a lush garden of rosebushes. Stimulate your senses by feeling, seeing, smelling, sensing and listening to the energy around you.

You may receive an audible message or just feel a loving touch. Ask a question while you meditate. Try to visualize or sense a spirit guide coming to you and giving you an answer. You might ask about your soul's purpose in this lifetime or what lessons you need to learn.

Meditation balanced with prayer puts you in touch with your own divine being and enables you to listen to promptings from your still inner voice.

4 - Doorways to the Spiritual World

Faithfully practicing prayer and meditation promotes a receptive mode that allows spiritual promptings and messages to come through for your highest good and for the highest good of humanity. Keep a journal when you pray and meditate. After each session, write down any insights you receive. You never know—writing or sharing your experiences may also help someone else seeking spiritual understanding.

The new millennium ushered in a more pronounced connection with the fourth dimension. Knowledge, experiences and information about spiritual portals are more common in this day and age. Communication with angels, spirit guides and the higher realms are now considered popular, and a spiked interest in the concept has captivated people all over the world. People are much more amenable to accepting and documenting this phenomenon than ever before.

Messages from the spiritual realm transpire in a multitude of ways. For some, these messages come during meditation or in the automatic writing that follows it. For others, insights come through the intuitive voice within— from dreams or visions. You might receive messages via so-called coincidental events and circumstances; while other times, angels or guides appear as apparitions while you're awake. They can even appear as messengers in the form of birds, butterflies or certain animals. There is also the possibility of words coming through out of nowhere that send comfort and guidance when trouble affects us or a person close to us.

Many souls are being called upon in some way by the creative forces to be a light, a helper or a guide for others who are in the beginning stages of awakening. The more time we dedicate on a daily basis to pray and meditate, the more information and assistance the higher beings can provide us. Do not be discouraged if revelations don't manifest immediately with prayer or meditation. Sometimes answers or insights happen when they are least expected. Give this your best shot by being open, receptive and aware. The more we make ourselves consciously available to be channels of blessings to others, the more gifts will be manifested through us.

The prayer of protection should be said before beginning any spiritual practice. The prayer ensures that any lower, earthbound forces that exist do not interfere.

Remember to pray and visualize the white light of the Christ Consciousness surrounding you.

5 - *Information on the 11:11 Concept*

Over the last two decades, I have personally been aware of the number 11:11 around me. For example, I would just happen to glance at the time in my home or car and see it was 11:11. I would randomly see 11:11 on license plates in front of me, on billboards and on addresses. Sometimes my purchases at different stores would ring up $11.11.

The frequency of seeing 11:11 prompted me to explore the significance behind the numbers. I came to realize I was not alone in this experience. Others began to share their personal stories with me about this number appearing in their lives. One such friend, who lives in Philadelphia and owns an Irish conglomerate of pubs, restaurants and stores, has seen 11:11 for years. He noticed that even the employees he hired were connected to the number. Many were born in November (the eleventh month of the year) or on the eleventh day of a month. A lot of other people also shared that they were experiencing an awareness of seeing 11:11 around them. That made me curious, so I started to delve deeper into the concept.

I contacted the angels that I work with, the light beings, in hopes of understanding more about this numerical occurrence. My research indicated the eleventh day of a month or the eleventh month of the year opens a portal of energy for meditation and prayer. November eleventh is a particularly powerful day. In fact, 11:11 represents pillars that open up to a higher vibration and bridge the gap between the dimensions. And 11:11 is a mirrored image that means "as above, so below." The numbers have to do with a mass consciousness shift that started accelerating in 2011. The shift prompts awareness by humanity that define what role we play in the universe. A gradual evolution into the next stage of mankind's development will occur. As a result, we will be vibrating at a higher frequency, working with mental telepathy and our perceptions and senses will be heightened. Connections to other worlds and beings will take place. And our destiny will progress faster with our thought forms. Certain souls incarnate on earth to serve as light workers who aid in raising the consciousness of humanity. These souls were evolving and closely linked to other dimensions before birth. They are here as "awakened ones" that help others to awaken as well. They are pre-coded, so to speak, with the numbers 11:11 in their auric field. Seeing 11:11 activates the soul's DNA and is a trigger in the cellular memory bank. Thus, 11:11 appears when you are ready for change and a new heightened spiritual energy.

Those that have been aware of 11:11 for years are helping others open up to their mission. Many of these light workers that are predestined to be physical, emotional or spiritual healers do not always remember their destiny. They often arrive at their life's purpose by questioning 11:11 since it is a trigger that helps them awaken. These souls are not necessarily confined to a full-time career in healing or psychic mediumship. Light workers help other souls intuitively every day. They are sensitive to other's feelings and give exemplary advice and guidance, even if it's just in passing.

The eleventh day of every month is an opportune time to create, design, heal, counsel or start new projects. It's a good day to receive guidance or clarity from your angels or guides through meditation, and it is an especially powerful day for prayer or doing metaphysical work. The 11:11 portal concept is about new opportunities, expansion, insights and shifts to come. When you see 11:11, it may just reveal that you're a light worker that is here to enlighten others and connect those around you with information and awareness of the higher realms. A sense of awakening or awareness is the essence of 11:11.

6 - *Messages from Automatic or Spontaneous Writing*

Automatic or spontaneous writing is an inspiring way to communicate with your angels, guides and departed loved ones. I suggest engaging in automatic writing when you're completely at peace. Quiet the mind and drown out any potential distractions. Be centered, focused and comfortable before beginning. I find that immediately following prayer or meditation is the perfect time to engage in this writing exercise because the mind and psyche are calm.

Create a sacred place in your home where you can relax for consistent communication, like a spare bedroom or a private corner of a room. Creating an altar can be beneficial in this process because it helps pull in the energy of your guides and angels. The altar allows an energy vortex to magnetize your guides to come through and communicate. Buy blank notebooks with light blue, lavender or white paper. Lavender opens the third eye, which is the seat of intuition; blue brings peace; and white promises protection.

After meditation, place your notebook in front of you on the altar. If you know your soul symbol, draw it in the upper left corner. If you know the name of your guide or angel, write it across the top of the paper (see the next chapter). Close your eyes and take a deep breath. Visualize pure white light surrounding your body, and say the following prayer:

> *Dear Lord, please protect me during this process. Let only those souls or energies for my highest good and the highest good of humanity come through. Let the information I receive come from a place of pure peace and love. Amen.*

It is of utmost importance that when you practice spiritual work, you protect and employ the white light technique. The unnerving fact remains that there are earthbound or discarnate spirits on the earth plane who sometimes get caught between the third and fourth dimensions. Some souls refuse to go to the light, and some are confused because they died tragically and can't find the light. While we should pray that these souls find their peace, you don't want them coming through and interrupting your writing or giving you advice that is not for your highest good.

Do not write under the influence of alcohol or recreational drugs. Doing so may cause information coming through to be tainted. Be a pure channel for your spirit guides and angels so that you are not driving a spiritual car without brakes, so to speak. If you're concerned about whether the information given to you is pure and for your best interests, look at the messages and trust your own intuition. If the advice is uplifting, good, practical and loving, you're in the presence of your guides and angels. If you wish, write a question at the top of the paper and wait. Let ideas gradually come into your mind as messages and insights emerge.

After preparing yourself, start writing. The words you write are not from your imagination or subconscious. They will be from your lifetime companion angel or a guide who may be a departed loved one. Your guide is a human soul who has lived on earth at some point in history and has trained to be your helper. Everyone has a prominent lifetime guide. Your companion angel is an androgynous light being that God created to assist your soul on its journey. A specific departed loved one can also speak to you if you write his or her name at the top of the paper.

Discipline yourself to write daily and it will become easier over time. You will be nothing short of amazed at the messages you receive. Ask for your spirit guide's or angel's name, and on future sessions write the name at the top of the paper; this will assist in pulling in their energy. If the spirit guide's last lifetime on the earth plane was in Egypt or ancient Greece, for example, the writing, verbiage or terminology may be slightly foreign to you. However, the differences and linguistic obstacles will work themselves out as you continue to work together on a routine basis, and communication lapses will dissipate in time.

Patience and persistence are instrumental to this process. Following my advice and the aforementioned techniques will open up a beautiful portal into the realms of the spirit world. Communication will be safe and effortless.

7 - Soul Color, Gemstone, Number and Symbol

Every soul vibrates with a particular color, gemstone, number and symbol. Discovering the color that your soul is connected to has the potential to empower you. Knowing your soul color can be as simple as picking your favorite shade or determining the color of clothing that you feel radiates positive energy when worn. It's the one color you want to surround yourself with that makes you feel good. Although we may change our thoughts, opinions and desires as we mature, the soul color has been a constant throughout our lives.

Intuition is often the guiding force that helps souls define their specific color. Frequently wearing dark, neutral colors like black, brown, gray or navy, can shrink the auric field and result in feeling tired, depressed or even ill. Most soul colors are jewel-like colors that vibrate with the upper chakra points of the body, from the heart region up to the top of the head. Jewel-like colors are emerald green, aqua or azure blue, teal, royal or cobalt blue, purple and white (the reflection of all colors). There are cases where individuals feel good with lower chakra colors, like sunny golden yellow, orange or red. However, wearing red consistently can make you hyper, excitable and nervous. Therefore, I suggest wearing lower chakra colors as wardrobe accents or as occasional alternates for fun. Men can apply soul color with their shirts, sweaters and ties.

Soul colors provide a sense of well-being and a feeling of peace. Each soul color has an accompanying gemstone, which is not necessarily your birthstone. When the gemstone is worn, it can also protect and energize your body and aura. The color white would be represented by a diamond or white pearl, purple by the amethyst, royal blue by the sapphire and aqua with the aquamarine or blue topaz. Green is represented by the emerald, yellow by the citrine and orange with a deep golden topaz, carnelian or amber. And, of course, red is represented by a ruby or garnet.

In addition to the color and gemstone, the soul is aligned with a number. This number is a dominant force in your life and can be linked to birth dates, addresses and phone numbers, to name a few. An affinity to a "lucky number" sometimes reveals the identity of a soul number.

The soul numeral is always a single digit and ranges from one to nine. Should you find yourself drawn to a double digit, add the numbers together and reduce them to a single digit. Take twenty-two for example; two plus two equals four, so the number four is the soul number. If you don't have a soul number already and no number jumps out at you immediately, just take the time to think about a recurring number that resonates with you. Trust me—you will be amazed at how your soul number appears throughout various facets of your life once you know what it is. Also, be cognizant of what happens on the day or month of your soul number. For example, if your soul number is three, watch for special events happening on the third day of the month or the third month of the year.

Lastly, discern a soul symbol. Most symbols are geometric shapes and correlate with soul numbers. They are usually circles, squares, rectangles, triangles, diamonds, hexagons, octagons, etc. For example, a triangle correlates with the number three because of its three sides. The square or rectangle correlates with the number four, and the octagon correlates with the number eight. Most of these can also be represented with a three-dimensional form that can be carried or placed in an area that is frequented. A circle becomes a ball, a triangle becomes a pyramid and so on. Sketch different shapes and see which one appeals to you. After deciding, you can incorporate the

siness cards, letterheads or your website. You
r it as jewelry.

figure out the vibrational color, gemstone,
symbol of your soul, it will align your entire
t you in touch with the magnificent person
ly are. Establishing a soul color, number,
l symbol completes the soul identity.

8 - *Astral Projection*

our souls embark on a journey to work, learn
ly grow on the earth plane, we continue to
r dimensions of light and energy while alive.
ally, our souls roam through dimensions
erience deep sleep at night. The soul travels
nally—a process referred to as "astral
here is an invisible silver cord attached to
body in the solar plexus region (similar to the
l) that is also attached to the midsection of
en your soul projects, the cord stretches.
l returns too quickly, the cord snaps back
into the body. So if you find yourself jerking awake at
times, that's the reason.

We may be met by spirit guides, angels or departed
loved ones in other dimensions. Members of our soul group
who are not incarnated at this time are also there to greet
us. Astral projecting allows the soul to access the Akashic
(soul) Records, be mentored by our guides and have the
opportunity to explore and travel through nine other
dimensions of light and energy. Most souls project two
nights a week. However, some souls are dedicated to astral
work and leave four or five nights a week. Astral traveling
too much can be taxing on the physical body and energy
levels.

There are three ways to determine if you've been astral
projecting. The first and most obvious indication is if you
don't dream or can't remember your dreams. Spiritual
amnesia results from astral traveling. We do not remember
our experiences unless we explicitly ask to. The second

sign is if you wake up restless between 3:00 and 5:00 A.M. and can't fall back asleep; that strongly suggests you left and reentered your body. Lastly, if you're exhausted or dizzy in the morning and slept an adequate amount, you most likely traveled. Occasional dreams of flying or falling may also be an indication of your explorations.

If you would like to remember these nightly journeys, just ask. Before turning in for the night, ask your "soul mind" to show you the other realms in lucid detail, and ask to consciously retain the experiences. Keep a notepad or recording device by your bed and immediately jot down or record your impressions as soon as you wake up.

There is a way to command your soul to stay in your body on certain nights. If there is something important that you need to do the next day (whether it's a meeting at work, a school exam or some other important activity), then this request is invaluable for energy and well-being. Say the following before you fall asleep:

I do not want my soul to leave my body tonight. I want to stay in my body, dream and experience rapid eye movements (REM). and I want to wake up fully refreshed with energy in the morning.

I recommend astral projection two or three nights a week. Some of our greatest work, both for ourselves and for humanity, is accomplished via astral projection. Balancing astral travel and deep sleep by alternating nights is a great way to maximize the benefits of both and reap the rewards they offer.

9 – Awareness of Soul Memory

We have all been on a long journey throughout eternity. God wants to experience the universe through us, and does so through our thought forms and actions. You may think of your soul as the driver and your body as the vehicle that is utilized to create your destiny. The soul, which is eternal and indestructible, retains its own mind, a distinct creating positive experiences through the things you love to do—your skills, your talents and your good qualities. Mozart (a child prodigy) started composing and playing the piano without any training at the age of three. This gift or talent was honed from past life experiences when the soul had the opportunity to learn these skills.

Conversely, if something shocking, traumatic or devastating occurs, negative experiences shape the soul memory. As an adult, you may be perpetuating these negative influences through fears, phobias, illnesses and addictive behaviors. These patterns are blocks that prevent forward progression on the spiritual journey and should be eradicated for soul advancement.

I frequently receive information about a client's fears or phobias during a reading. To tackle the issue at its core, we venture back to the past life that created the traumatic experience. Although this process is emotionally taxing and mentally grueling, it is a vital step to ensure the wellness of the individual. Without fail, once the soul acknowledges the truth, the phobia immediately leaves.

With my third eye, I see these fears as black talons, or hooks, that are embedded in a person's soul body. One client, for example was claustrophobic and could not venture near an elevator, a closet or a basement. She also slept with the lights turned on. It was revealed in the reading that the client was falsely accused of a crime and imprisoned in the Tower of London during a past life. She was sentenced to a dark dungeon and placed in a small iron box, unable to stretch or stand. The guards left her in that horrendous condition without food or water for three days. The trauma of that experience was a negative hook that became ingrained in her soul memory. In this present lifetime, the past life shock perpetuated obsessive claustrophobia. Once she realized the reason behind her fear, the soul acknowledged the trauma and released it and the claustrophobia was gone.

Another female client, who had both a fear of cats and smothering to death, had an Egyptian lifetime as an architect who designed the pyramids. After the pharaoh's death, she was buried alive along with the pharaoh's cats and other servants. As the oxygen slowly decreased in the sunken, dark burial chamber, panic set in. The cats clawed at the walls and attacked the entombed servants. Thus, the last memory my client had was the suffocating darkness, the piercing howls of the cats and their scratching claws. When this devastating experience was brought to her conscious attention, her phobias immediately left. She now has two kitties that she adores, and her fear of suffocating is gone.

I have seen and helped clients overcome emotional issues time and again. Once past life traumas are realized, the soul releases them. Take a moment to think of your own fears. What scares you? If you do not remember any childhood experience that could account for the phobia, it may stem from a past life experience. Examine the themes or patterns of fears that have been present throughout

, ...and deeds. We can never run away from ourselves, and as it says in the Bible, "We must face ourselves in a mirror dimly lit." This self-evaluation takes place during a "life review."

There are a few people who have experienced a near death experience (NDE), who were considered clinically dead and have recounted their life review experience with others. Since time does not exist in other dimensions, many recall seeing their lives flash before them in what can be described as a few seconds or minutes. According to these same people, upon arrival in the fourth dimension, the soul is escorted to a way station where the life review occurs. It appears to us as a third dimensional hologram or movie. We relive and experience all of our feelings, thoughts and emotions from the time of our first breath to the very last moment we spend alive. We objectively become aware of the loving, thoughtful, positive and encouraging things we did for others, no matter how grand or miniscule. We become more aware and feel the individuals' joy and happiness, realizing exactly how we've touched others' lives

Every action is observed and analyzed in an unbiased way. We experience the abuse and hurtful emotions we inflicted on others, even if we were not consciously aware of them while alive. We briefly feel the other person's emotional pain. Although we do not feel their physical pain, we are introduced to the emotional anguish and devastation they have felt. The past life review is crucial for soul growth. It instills a significant sense of compassion for other souls around us. It also makes us aware that even one simple action can have a ripple effect on humanity.

After the information is processed, the Creator will ask, "What do you have to show me for your life?" This question is aimed at addressing the fulfillment of your soul purpose. You will then respond. Thereafter, the ultimate question will be asked, and it is quite simple, yet profound: How have you loved? The soul journey is about unconditional love. By answering this question, we evaluate ourselves and examine what we learned in that lifetime. God is a source of pure unconditional love and light and we are here to try to manifest this love in our every thought and action. This is our birthright because God is within each one of us.

Finally, a counsel of souls meets with us to discuss the virtues we have learned. These souls work with us to determine if we have accomplished our soul mission for that lifetime. We then decide how we need to proceed and progress. We can stay in the fourth dimension to learn and grow soulwise, or we can be born into a new human body in the third dimension to learn more lessons. For this decision, the life review is as insightful as it is invaluable. Forgiveness enters into this concept as well. We need to forgive ourselves as we forgive others. Consider this idea in your daily dealings with yourself as well as with others. Think about the welfare and feelings of everyone, and aspire in a gentle and kind way to make the world a better place.

Creating An
Organizing

Relating
Children

Writing

Coordinator

Flexib

a

co

hac

othe

E

a slig

choosh

bedridd

do put (me)

sometime

hand, whe

accident, i

sometimes e

light without

coming for the

departed friend

belief systems (...,, we perpetuate with
our thought for .. what we believe immediately upon
arrival on the other side. For example, a Christian may see
Jesus, a Catholic may see the saints and Mother Mary, a
Buddhist may see Buddha and so on. This occurs after the
soul travels through the tunnel to the fourth dimension.

When we finally breathe our last breath, the soul exits
through the top of the head, rises above the body and
sometimes looks back at the lifeless shell left behind. We
rapidly travel, or float, through the connecting portal, or
tunnel, to the fourth dimension. Many have described this
tunnel as a dark spiral with bright rainbow sparkles. The
fourth dimension is filled with love, bright light, peace,
beautiful music and extraordinary colors. At the end of the
tunnel, we are greeted by angels of transition who assist us
further along. We are met by our departed loved ones,
friends and even companion pets. Our spirit guides may
also appear.

Your soul will then start to adjust to the higher and faster frequency of the fourth dimension. Some souls attend their own funeral or memorial by pulling their energy down to the third dimension. Those who do not believe in any form of life after death may sleep or cocoon for a while until they are gently awakened by their guides and angels. If these souls still denounce where they are, they go back to the cocoon stage once more. There is no time as we know it in the fourth dimension; therefore, a soul could sleep for many years. Then, with gentle and patient prodding, these sleeping nonbelievers awaken and accept the fact that there is another realm that is very real. It is then that is when their life review begins.

Some souls go to a play neutral area for the soul's rehabilitation process and evaluation before the life review. This is a special area for those who have died in some traumatic situation, such as a drug overdose, a violent suicide or combat. This is not a negative or judgmental area but a place of regrouping for those who have been tormented or felt lost before they passed.

God loves all souls and accepts all back into His arms of love. We need to take responsibility, though, and consciously be aware of our thoughts and actions while we are alive. Souls like Saddam Hussein or Hitler are very young souls, filled with ego and wanting absolute power. These entities that killed and tortured so many are still loved by God and given a chance to rectify their actions. But these souls must first recognize and grasp the light. Through regrouping in the next realm, they eventually awaken to the truth and acknowledge a higher power, and then their life review begins. Our prayers for troubled souls help them tremendously, especially those that have had a difficult time during their life on earth. There is hope for every created soul, for the soul of each individual is innately pure.

After the life review, we decide how we want our soul to progress. There are just as many things to do on the other side as there are on the earth plane. For example, there are temples of wisdom and learning where we can spiritually develop. We can choose to work with other souls who sit on councils to influence global peace and healing. Issues such as poverty, starvation, crime and environmental concerns can be addressed. A soul can choose to learn about the arts, music, science, literature or philosophy.

An important work that some of our deceased loved ones do on the other side is working with rescue angels. This is a group of angelic beings combined with souls just like us, who assist in accident situations on the earth plane. Many of us can recall situations where there were "close calls"—where we were nearly in a traumatic accident and yet were inexplicably saved from being hurt or killed. Chances are the rescue angels were overseeing the situation. They don't always intervene. Sometimes angels of transition are present to help souls out of the physical realm and into the spiritual realm. Regardless of the way a loved one passes over to the spirit world, they are always in the companionship of guardian angels.

Many souls do not want to immediately study or progress, but wish to "kick back" and enjoy themselves for a little while. It's wonderful to know that we can create our own heavens through our thought forms. Even things like gardens, forests, mansions, kitchens (though we can't eat or drink) or our favorite recliner can be manifested.

Eventually we become tired of lounging and get serious about soul progression. Again, there is no timeline for this. At this point, some souls choose to reincarnate into a physical body and continue to learn lessons and skills on the earth plane. So with our spirit guide's help, we seek out and choose a set of parents to learn and grow with, and the cycle of the soul's evolution on earth begins once again.

12 - *Eradicating Psychic Attacks*

The negative energy that someone else puts out into the universe can directly affect our lives. Someone who may be angry at you or jealous of you can send you negative vibrations through their thought forms. These destructive thoughts can be sent to you regardless of where the other person is. People sending you these harmful thoughts may be confused or frustrated, have mental problems or be substance abusers who possess scattered energy. A series of negative events can happen for a number of reasons. At times, they are brought on by our own stress or need to learn spiritual lessons. And sometimes these occurrences are directed at us from others.

Psychic attacks from others tend to manifest rapidly, and assaults can include frequent accidents, lawsuits or hurtful situations that involve you, your family, pets, home or possessions. There may also be physical symptoms of psychic attacks. These can include dull pain in the solar plexus region, heart palpitations, a feeling of heaviness in the body or lower extremities or a feeling of dread. You may also experience mild nausea, headaches or recurring nightmares. While some people feel disturbing physical symptoms or experience negative situations, there are cases where all of these occurrences happen at one time, creating total incapacitation for the individual. Psychic attacks happen quickly, perpetuate a series of negative events and may display physical discomfort that is consistently located in certain regions of the body.

Be aware that there is a difference between an "attached spirit" (or a "cling-on" as they are sometimes called) and a psychic attack directed at you from someone else. How can you tell the difference? A discarnate spirit is one who is caught between our third-dimensional earth plane and the spiritual realms of the fourth dimension. A soul may be totally unaware that he or she has left his or her physical body and is still clinging to the earth plane. A traumatic or quick soul exit from an accident or murder may precipitate such a situation. (Think of the movie *Ghost* when Patrick Swayze didn't know he was dead.)

Some spirits are in denial and can't grasp the concept of an afterlife. Because of ego, they choose to ignore the light and are unaware of their angels and guides. A discarnate spirit can attach itself to you when you unknowingly open yourself up while dabbling in the spirit realms without protection or without using white lighting techniques. For example, you are courting with danger when you use the Ouija board without prayers or protection. In addition, there are many more innocent ways you may sometimes attract a discarnate spirit, such as when you are severely depressed, when you have experienced a serious injury or when you are under anesthesia.

When you have an attached spirit, you might display unusual behavior or engage in different personality traits than normal. Strange food cravings, excessive alcohol consumption or an irresistible urge to try drugs or start smoking may be signs a discarnate spirit is attached to you. These uncontrollable desires can become frustrating for the person feeling them. The attached spirit wants to vicariously live through them and use them to feel the physical world. An example could be that of an alcoholic. A soul like this could choose not to go to the light but hover around bars waiting for someone to pass out and then enter their body to feel the effects of alcohol. Of course, this is only true in some cases. Some may experience dizziness or throw spontaneous temper tantrums. A malevolent entity of this nature can be removed through hypnosis or other spiritual practices.

First, if you suspect you are under psychic attack, stop and think about what has transpired with your relationships recently. Did you terminate a friendship that had become draining? Did you break off an intimate relationship that was confining or controlling? Did you become involved with someone new who you're not sure of? Have your interactions with others been antagonistic or conflicting in any way? Do you suspect jealousy, envy or anger from someone around you? Someone who is not for your highest good may have recently entered your workspace, neighborhood or environment. You will find that the timing of your attacks may coincide with relationship changes that have taken place. In some cases, you may not even know the person sending you these vibes.

There are two current cases of psychic attacks that come to mind. First, I counseled a client (who I will call Mary) under siege. Mary became nervous, anxious and frightened. She even felt physically ill. Mary admitted that she had befriended someone new via the Internet (who I will call Sarah). Sarah was a substance abuser from a dysfunctional family who needed emotional support, and Mary felt compelled to oblige. Sarah became very dependent on Mary's advice, and since Mary "needed to be needed," it created a codependent relationship. After a few months, Mary could no longer take the intense emotional drain and responsibility for Sarah's life and cut off communication. A few days later, Mary distanced herself from this Internet stranger, and the attacks began.

Apparently, Sarah also had some mental problems and felt extremely angry and obsessively betrayed. Even though Sarah lived on the West Coast and Mary lived on the East Coast, the attacks continued because thoughts and energy are not confined to a limited space.

Another client, Sue, had her unstable sister visit from Europe for the holidays. Sue's sister was a drug addict and an envious person who was jealous of Sue's husband, children, farm and lifestyle. She asked Sue for money, which Sue declined to give her for personal reasons. After her sister left and went back to Europe, the psychic attacks started. Over the course of two weeks, Sue's husband and son were in a near fatal car accident, Sue had a car accident and her champion show horse became ill. To make matters worse, plumbing problems in her home had caused serious damage.

Be aware that the attacker may not even consciously know they are hurting you with their thoughts. In both of these cases, it was advised to do a cord-cutting exercise to dispel the attacks.

If you find that you may be the target of these attacks, it is imperative to break free of them. First, try to pinpoint the person who is attacking you. Lie down, close your eyes and visualize the attacker's face, heart region and solar plexus region in your mind's eye. Imagine a dark red cord extending from the middle of their forehead to your forehead. Now see a thick dark red cord extending from their heart to your heart and a cord from their solar plexus region to yours. These cords bind the negative energy that is being sent to you, and they need to be cut. If you cannot pinpoint who is attacking you, visualize a silhouette in front of you and use it to do the exercise.

Next, call upon Archangel Michael, the divine protector, to assist you with the cord-cutting process. Visualize a very large pair of golden shears. Hold the shears and visualize the cords attached to you from the attacker, and say the following:

With God's divine protection, I now cut the negative cords and thoughts sent to me from you. The cords are cut from my mind, heart and soul. You can no longer harm me, for I am surrounded by God's pure white light of love and protection. I now dispel any future psychic attacks or negative karmic ties to anyone, and I live in peace, safety and love.

See the attachments severed and falling away. Do this exercise a few times a day and before you go to sleep at night. Almost immediately after doing them, you will start to feel better and stronger. You will begin to see positive changes and improvements in your life within a few days.

Part III: Spiritual and Metaphysical Concepts

Very few metaphysical concepts presented in the following chapters are backed by scientific knowledge or proof. They are, however, based on clinical and personal experiences I have encountered over the last twenty years. Most of the ideas have been gained through insights during meditation and from my three light beings. The light beings are evolved solar angels who tap into universal knowledge and assist me during readings.

Hopefully, the spiritual knowledge presented here will give you a new enlightened perspective on the evolution of your soul, your physical body and the glorious world you inhabit. It is my greatest wish that this guided information helps you remove any blinders and encourages you to passionately explore your own spiritual journey.

1-Colors of the Chakra Points

The human aura is comprised of seven major points of color, also known as the chakras. Chakra comes from Sanskrit, the ancient language of India, and means "wheel of energy." Every person has seven endocrine glands that regulate body functions; those points are where the chakras are located. Energy flows in and out of these chakra centers.

All human beings are walking "prisms of light" and come from the pure white light of the fourth dimension. The white light is a result of all the colors of the spectrum combined. You may have noticed religious pictures depicting halos above Jesus, Mary and different saints. These halos are representative of the light emanating from the tops of their heads. I highly recommend wearing white if you feel negativity; the color protects and expands the aura.

The very top of the head is the Crown Chakra. Violet, or purple, vibrates at the Crown Chakra, where the pineal gland is located. Violet represents higher learning and spiritual wisdom. Wearing this color helps one's intuition. Plus, it's a great remedy for reducing headaches. The Crown Chakra is stimulated when the gemstone amethyst is worn.

As you make your way down from the Crown Chakra, the next region is the forehead area, also defined as the Brow Chakra. The pituitary gland is located here. This is also where the third eye, or the seat of intuition, sits. An indigo blue color is the vibration for the Brow Chakra. Wearing royal blue helps clairvoyance and telepathy. The accompanying gemstone to this chakra is sapphire.

The next wheel of energy is the Throat Chakra. The thyroid gland is located in this area, and bright blue is the color associated here. I always encourage individuals who use their voice for a living—teachers, counselors, lecturers, singers, stage actors, etc.—to wear aqua. Blue is good for stress reduction and helps energize the throat and vocal cords. Aquamarine and blue topaz are the designated gemstones of the Throat Chakra, and they are excellent energizers.

The next chakra center is the Heart Chakra. This area embodies the seat of emotions. Emerald green is the color of this chakra. Green is the color of nature and balances the lower and higher chakra points. It has also been studied and endorsed as a healing color, a reason why many hospital rooms are painted green. Emeralds, malachite and peridot can be worn to invigorate the Heart Chakra.

The Solar Plexus Chakra is the next chakra on the body. It is located in the naval area, where the adrenal glands are found. Many people hold fear and stress in this region of the body. Bright yellow is the color for the Solar Plexus Chakra. Yellow energizes the midsection of the body along with that area's internal organs. It also stimulates brain cells and can help us remember details. The accompanying gemstone is yellow citrine. Gold is the metal that protects the solar plexus.

Below the solar plexus is the Spleen Chakra. The pancreas and the elimination system (kidney, bladder and intestines) are located here. Wearing orange revitalizes this region and helps with elimination. The gemstones associated with the Spleen Chakra are golden topaz, amber and carnelian.

The last chakra point is the Root Chakra. This chakra is located at the base of the spine, or coccyx region, and it stimulates the reproductive organs. Red is the color of health, vitality and passion; it correlates with the Root Chakra. When worn, red speeds up metabolism and is good for weight loss. If red is worn too often, however, the color can cause hyper behavior or nervousness. I recommend wearing this shade sparingly. Rubies, garnets and coral are stones that stimulate this chakra.

Our auric fields are highly susceptible to the energy of the colors we wear. Dark neutral colors—brown, black, gray and navy—shrink the auric field. To spiritually expand the aura, wear emerald green, aqua, indigo blue, violet and white.

2 - Souls who Came to the Earth Plane from the Stars

Not all souls incarnate to the earth plane each time; some incarnate to star belt planes for higher learning and development. The star belts of Pleiades, Orion and Sirius are just a few examples of areas in the galaxy where souls are born.

Sensitive beings born on earth from these higher realms are called "star children," or "hybrid souls." Star children do not like loud abrasive people and can't stand bright, harsh lights or loud, discordant music. Often, these souls seek places of peace and quiet. There are many meditation chambers in the star belts, and incarnated souls from these regions seek to bring compassion and love to our world. Even though they are peaceful in nature, these souls are strong and manifest their purpose and mission in their own way. Typical responses of star children include "Nobody can tell them what to do!" or "They are going to have their own way, or else!" These souls have a mind and will of their own. Star children are free spirits and can't be controlled.

You may know a child or person of this temperament. With children, it's very important to allow their creative gifts to manifest naturally. These souls are spiritually evolved, and many will become leaders and teachers in areas of spiritual thought if they are nurtured properly. Those who come from the stars are able to "go with the flow" and handle changes easier than others. When encountering an obstacle, these souls find a way to deal with the issue effortlessly; no challenge is too big for star children.

Nature is a big part of star children. They are innately attuned to the nature kingdom and often feel closest to the universe when they are outdoors. Whether they are observing butterflies, taking in the beauty of the flowers or resting by a tree, they feel complete when immersed in nature.

Another defining characteristic of star children is their ability to see the phenomenon of other realms. It's not uncommon for these children to see nature spirits like fairies, gnomes and elementals. Everyone has the capacity to be sensitive to these spirits, but star children are naturally aware of them very early on due to their heightened sensitivity.

People from star realms who incarnate to the earth are often artists, dancers, musicians, writers, speakers and singers. They are drawn to the arts because of their heightened sensitivity. Many of the souls that incarnate from these realms are different from the rest of their family; they frequently feel like an outcast.

If you are a parent to one of these highly evolved souls, you are blessed with an extremely gifted child. With loving care and nurturing attention, these children can grow to greatly impact the world. Their interest in books, movies and the arts might seem unusual, but encourage your child to explore the things they love. Help by explaining to them that they are unique and that God proudly made them that way. Support your child's uniqueness and individuality by maintaining an open relationship. Remind them that they are loved, safe and normal. Without proper guidance, these sensitive souls can become withdrawn or depressed, and most are susceptible to feeling isolated. Many parents and adults in these modern times are star children as well. If you feel like you don't fit in, you could be one of these highly evolved souls.

Earth life is difficult for star people, but they come to this plane to learn important lessons about being human. Due to the highly sensitive realms star souls journeyed from, living on earth poses several challenges. But earth is temporary. Their true home is among the celestial regions; they are here to evolve their souls just like every other soul.

Do not be discouraged if you feel like you have identified yourself as a star person. You are blessed and overseen by higher beings, and your presence on earth is vital for everyone. Not only will your own soul develop greatly while on earth, but you will impact the development of others around you. When you feel alone, seek the peace that comes from meditating. In the silence of your soul and spirit, seek quiet time and ask for strength, guidance and direction from our Creator. Rest assured that you will be given what you ask for. Remember that you have a high mission and purpose in the earth realm now and that your presence is seriously needed. Take time every day to pray and meditate, and cherish God's divinity. From within, you will be given the understanding and wisdom that the world cannot give you. In time, you will find your own true peace.

3 - The Twelve Dimensions

Over the last two decades, my three light beings have shared information with me on the twelve dimensions.

They have the ability to tap into universal knowledge and have provided me with knowledge about the other dimensions. Think of the analogy of someone throwing a pebble into a lake and watching concentric circles emerge. The godhead is the pebble, so to speak—the center of all creation. The concentric circles represent the dimensions that emanate from the Creator. Thus, they are not linear (like a ladder) but overlapping dimensions in a spiral form and in unison.

The twelfth dimension is the Creator's celestial kingdom. It was in this dimension that the many universes, plants, life forms and souls were conceived. God is a powerful energy source of pure unconditional love, light and wisdom, and we as human souls are sparks of that source.

I have also learned that the eleventh dimension emanates from God and houses the hierarchies of angels, or light beings. Angels have never been human souls, although they can take on a human form when necessary. A guardian angel was created to oversee and protect each human soul for all eternity. There are different categories of angels that work with humans, animals, plants or the four elements—earth, air, fire and water.

Supposedly, there are nine realms of angels in the hierarchy of the eleventh dimension. They include the Seraphim (who vibrate with unconditional love), the Cherubim (who are the guardians of wisdom), the Thrones (who represent the scales of balance), the Dominions (who work with the will of God), the Virtues (who work with miracles), the Powers (who keep a check on negativity), the Principalities (who guard national leaders and religions), the Archangels (who are the messengers and protectors) and finally the Angels (who deal with mankind).

Angels who work specifically with humans have designated roles. For example, birthing angels are sent to assist our souls when we enter our baby body with our first breath. Project angels help us with building a home, writing a book or other creative endeavors. Healing angels are sent to us when we are ill to give us peace and comfort.

And guardian angels never leave our side and protect us in every living moment. Truly evolved souls inhabit the tenth dimension. These souls, through many incarnations on the earth plane and advancements in other dimensions, have progressed to the point of pure love and wisdom. Examples of these souls are great ascended masters, saints, prophets, avatars, sages and gurus. This vast group of entities can tap into universal knowledge and mentor those in other realms with their wealth of wisdom. Universal truths are known to those in the tenth dimension.

The ninth dimension houses extraterrestrial life forms from other universes, planets and galaxies. These life forms are not human souls, but different groups of collective energy or consciousness. The extraterrestrial life forms travel through other dimensions at lightning speed. As a result, sightings of ETs appear to us and rapidly disappear. Humans are constantly being observed on the third dimension by these other life forms. ETs do not wish to be born in our dense third-dimensional world, but they want to observe it. Similarly, they do not wish to harm humans. However, they have abducted people in order to study human DNA and diversified personalities.

In our immediate universe, there is a star belt known as the Pleiades, which makes up the eighth dimension. Here, a collective consciousness of Pleiadians reside. Their communication is telepathic, or mind-to-mind. The teachings in their star system are of healing, love, shape shifting and spirituality. They can incarnate to our third-dimensional realm as star children. The Pleiadians have meditation chambers, where they resonate with the vibrations of the color spectrum and harmonic chords of sound. Air and water are the primary elements of this star system, and shades of blue are the primary colors. Our "dolphin consciousness" here on the earth plane is said to have come from Pleiades. These sea mammals are highly evolved and communicate with unique sounds and via telepathy.

Pleiadians incarnate to our dimension to bring to us unconditional love. They usually incarnate into dysfunctional family units to get a crash course about human souls. They have very expressive eyes, beautiful features and are gentle peace bringers. They also love nature and many times get involved with global issues such as poverty, starvation and the environment. The Pleiadians telepathically mentored some of the great classical artists, architects, sculptors and philosophers of ancient Greece.

The eighth dimension overlaps and merges with other star belts in the seventh dimension like Orion, Sirius and Arcturus. As the Pleiadians mentored the ancient Greek cultures, the Orions mentored all ancient civilizations that used pyramidal structures—the Aztecs, Mayans, Egyptians and Atlantians. All civilizations were guided in some way by the seventh dimension. For example, astronomers in Egypt aligned the three pyramids of Giza to correlate with the alignment of the three stars of Orion's belt.

The sixth dimension is comprised of the fairy/deva and elemental kingdoms. Fairies, or devas, oversee the growth and development of the earth's trees, flowers and plants. If you have a flowering houseplant, examine each tiny bud carefully. When the plant blooms, know that it has been the direct result of the nurturing devas who surround it. Fairies help with the germination of all plant life throughout our third-dimensional world.

The elementals are spirits of the four main elements— earth, air, fire and water. Spirits of the air are called sylphs. Spirits of the earth are pixies or gnomes. Sprites and undines are the spirits that work with water (many people actually see them in waterfalls). And the spirits of the fire flames are called salamanders. Native Americans called on the sprites or undines for rain when they performed a rain dance. They also worked with salamanders when they danced in a circle around an open fire. Keep in mind that all of these dimensions overlap, so the sixth dimension of devas and elementals is constantly with us. We cannot always see or perceive these other dimensions because they are in a much higher and faster frequency than we are, and that is true of all dimensions from the fourth up through the twelfth.

The fifth dimension houses the records of all souls, also known as the Akashic Records. This documentation has captured and retains every detail of the soul's progression. From inception to the eternal and infinite rest with God, the Akashic Records are used as a reference to document the evolution of the soul. *Akasha* is a Sanskrit word meaning "a form of energy that is capable of storing the memories of life." Every thought, motivation, action, emotion or event that a human soul has experienced is housed within these records.

The Akashic Records can be accessed after death, when the soul travels to the heavenly realms of the fourth dimension. Spiritual entities guard the information contained therein. With permission, spirit guides can access the records to assist a soul along its evolutionary progression. But there are several other reasons to utilize the records. It is helpful to tap into the *Akasha* when a soul is choosing a new incarnation. The records influence decisions such as determining a new set of parents, sex, race or ethnic background. The *Akasha* are also invaluable in understanding what virtue a soul needs to master. If negativity is the result of a past or current life trauma, the records can be accessed for information needed to help a soul overcome the obstacles that result from it. Think of the fifth dimension as a hard drive that has infinitely recorded and stored everything—past, present and future.

The Akashic Records can also be accessed during astral traveling (when the soul temporarily leaves the body while sleeping). Before you go to bed, I recommend asking your spirit guides to help you recall the experiences during your sleep. Keep a notepad and pen by your bedside to write down any impressions or insights you receive.

The fourth dimension is where, for now, our departed loved ones and pets reside. This dimension is what many refer to as heaven. According to my light beings, there are three distinct levels of the fourth dimension. The lower level is comprised of souls who did not believe in any form of an afterlife or who have committed heinous crimes during their lifetime. Sometimes these souls cocoon until they have been spiritually rehabilitated enough for their life review. This lower level is a gray, neutral area, and it may take a soul hundreds of years to awaken or grasp the light and move on.

The next level of the fourth dimension is for disoriented souls who are confused about their transition. Sudden deaths, comas resulting in death or suicides may direct souls to this level of the fourth dimension. These souls are immediately welcomed into God's open arms, but must first be made aware of their location and accept that they have left the earth realm. Angels, guides and departed relatives gently help them. There is no condemnation in the fourth dimension. We judge our own soul's growth and development through the life review. This second level is just a short "way station" until these souls adjust to the higher and faster frequencies of the fourth dimension.

The third, or final, level is where most souls immediately go after dying unless they need to awaken, rest or rehabilitate. The life review occurs here, and souls have the ability to create what they want through thought forms. Everyone in this dimension looks about the age of thirty. Since the soul is electromagnetic energy, it can take on a pleasing appearance. We create our own "heavens" through our thoughts. If your grandma loved to garden, for example, she'll create a lush garden to inhabit. If your mother loved to cook, she may create a kitchen, even though we can't eat or drink in heaven. We also meet up with deceased friends, relatives and pets to exchange love with them. There are no negative emotions or thought forms here; everything is of the light.

We eventually lose the desire to recreate earthly memories and long to learn in temples of wisdom or science. Some souls choose to create beauty in schools of art, music, literature or philosophy. Other souls work with those still living on the earth plane or even train to be a "spirit guide" for another human being in the third dimension.

There are just as many things to do in the fourth dimension as there are in the third, if not more. The fourth dimension also has its communication and travel perks. We converse telepathically with all other souls; there is no language barrier. We can also choose to reenter the earth plane through reincarnation to learn soul lessons. As far as organized religion is concerned, the gates of heaven are wide, and there is no universal or right religion. As long as we have love in our hearts for God, our fellowman and ourselves, we can enter into this kingdom.

The third dimension is where we are now. It is a living and breathing world of plants, animals and humans. Our earthly realm is the densest inhabitable dimension of all twelve dimensions. The earth plane is a training ground to rapidly learn soul lessons and master certain virtues. Everyone is on a mission, whether they know it consciously or not. We all have a form of amnesia when we are born, and so the earthly journey is about rediscovering ourselves and learning why we are here. Free choice and free will allow the soul to choose its parents, sex, place and time of birth and physical death. In this dimension there are extreme polarities of light and dark, or positive and negative, energies that make staying focused difficult. Awareness is the one essential concept that contributes to successfully navigating through the earth plane. Take to heart and soul that we are all one, united in love, and honoring the animal and nature kingdoms with reverence.

Love is the single largest contributing component to promote soul growth and evolution. Tempered with wisdom and compassion, love nourishes the mind, body, soul and spirit like no other emotion is capable of doing. When we can reach the consciousness of an ascended master, like Christ, for example, we no longer need to reincarnate. We then reside in the tenth dimension with other ascended ones and no longer have a need for a physical body.

The second dimension is the energy of the rock and mineral kingdom and does not have a highly known consciousness. Souls do not incarnate to this dimension. Those of you who are jewelry designers or geologists or use crystals for healing are definitely working with the second dimension. The healing properties of gemstones and crystals are endless, and the wealth of knowledge being discovered from the offerings of this kingdom is far reaching. Wearing quartz crystals, for example, guards against stress and clears away negative energy. And placing a piece of quartz crystal under your pillow helps you to remember dreams.

The first dimension is also uninhabitable. This dimension is composed of dense, heavy energy with a thick molecular structure. Although all of the twelve dimensions are infinite and overlapping, the first dimension is the gravity of the universe, the neutral black hole of all existence. It is what eternally is between existences; it is the pause between thoughts and the binding strand that runs through all that is.

4 - The Golden Screw Protection Technique

All healing practitioners, from massage therapists to Reiki masters, need to protect themselves against the emotionally and physically draining work they may encounter. Departed souls and spirit guides inhabit a faster frequency that human souls are not accustomed to. Healers that tap into different realms are susceptible to the energies they comprise. The golden screw technique is a wonderful way to enable healers to open up to the spirit realms so that they can focus on healing without exhausting their bodies and minds. The technique also ensures a successful shutdown after a session to avoid further communication with or intrusion from other dimensions.

If you are a healing practitioner, implement the golden screw technique before beginning any work. Start the process by having your client close their eyes, and then close yours. In unison, take eight slow, deep breaths. Tell your client to visualize a blank wall while breathing to clear their energy. Then, visualize your own Crown Chakra. Imagine a large golden screw embedded at the top of your head. Slowly remove the screw and watch the bright white light pour into your Crown Chakra. Do the same visualization (with golden screws and white light) at your third-eye region (located about an inch above your eyebrows in the middle of your forehead), your Throat Chakra, Heart Chakra and solar plexus, as well as the palms of your hands and soles of your feet. The technique can be achieved successfully by the end of eight deep breaths. Upon completion, you will be spiritually open to other dimensions, but protected, and your client will be relaxed.

At the end of the session, make sure your client closes their eyes and rests. At this time, you should visualize the protective golden screws returning to each energy portal and chakra point. You are now closed down but energized and should not feel drained.

Try this exercise a few times and let it become part of your routine. You will find that this helps you to feel more relaxed while simultaneously creating protective boundaries.

5 - *Making Soul Agreements before Incarnating*

God created human souls long ago and still continues to create new ones. Consequently, there is a great variance in soul ages. Some souls are younger and more immature because they have had fewer earthly lifetimes in which to learn lessons. While alive and in the third dimension, young souls may exhibit behavior that is selfish, egotistical, materialistic or abusive. Yet, they are on a journey to learn wisdom, compassion and unconditional love. Some souls are older and have matured through different lifetimes. Certain souls may have studied and learned lessons in other dimensions of light as well. When the soul reaches the status of the Christ Consciousness, a saint or a guru, it is unlikely that reincarnation is chosen or needed for progression. At that point, the soul stays in the tenth dimension.

As God created souls, some magnetized together as they sparked from Him and formed soul groups. These souls sometimes congregated in teams of up to five hundred or more and elected to enter the earth plane together. The people around you are soul-connected to you —friends, relatives, spouses and even co-workers—and have been with you before at some point in history. And the relationships with the souls can vary significantly depending on the life lesson or purpose. We have effortless and fruitful bonds with some souls we're grouped with, while we struggle in other relationships because of past karmic cords that need to be remedied. Forgiveness is crucial for soul advancement, so forgive those who have wronged you in any way. Forgiveness will cut the negative cord that attaches your soul to theirs.

Before we choose an earthly body, we make agreements with other souls to decide how we will incarnate together and determine soul roles. Sometimes relatives that we've never met while alive, like great-grandparents, choose to become our guides from the other side. They agree to watch over us for our whole lifetime until we rejoin them in the heavenly realms of the fourth dimension. Thanks to free will, we dictate our life's pattern and choose our soul mates before we enter the earth plane.

6 - *Miscarriages, Stillborns, Abortions and Premature Death*

The loss of a child is one of the hardest challenges of earthly life. Many mothers experience a deep sense of guilt when they have a miscarriage or a stillborn baby or when the child lives only a few days or years. Those who experience the loss of a child ask, "Why me? What did I do wrong? Am I being punished?" Such experiences do not occur because of an error on the part of the parents. The reality is that the soul chooses everything.

If you have personally suffered the loss of a child, take into account that your child had a soul that chose a specific path. People often fear death, but it is much more difficult to be born into this world than it is to leave it. The soul leaves through the top of the head upon death, rises and goes through the tunnel into the fourth dimension. When we enter a new baby body, we come from the light through the tunnel and into the delivery room, watching (from an aerial view) our little baby bodies being born. We're pulling masses of soul memory and knowledge in at that point, and we can even change our minds after we see our baby bodies being born.

When we are born on earth, we are leaving the beautiful, light-filled realms of the fourth dimension, where there is no crime, war, negativity, abuse or pain. When our soul elects to enter the third dimension, we are actively agreeing to come into the material world to learn important lessons for growth and development. The decision is not easy, and complications in the transition can arise. There are occasions when the soul changes its mind, either just before or immediately after birth or within the first few years of life.

Miscarriage

The soul chooses its mother before conception and hovers around her during the period of pregnancy. If the soul changes its mind and chooses to remain in the spirit realms during the first few months of pregnancy, a miscarriage can result. The soul will then regroup and eventually select another time, place and possibly a new set of parents in which to incarnate.

Stillborn

The soul doesn't enter the body until the first breath is taken—*the breath of life.* A stillborn situation is when the baby body has come to full term and is delivered. The soul hovers above the body in the delivery room, looks down and says, "No, I've changed my mind. I can't, or don't want to, be born now." Stillborn is similar to miscarriage, only the physical body is fully developed. We have free choice in our third-dimensional world, just as in the heavenly realms, because our souls are within us.

Abortion

A woman can reject the pregnancy of a soul that wants to come through by having an abortion. The timing may not be right for her to be pregnant, or she may be doubting the character of her partner. The decision to say no to a pregnancy may even come from a devastating situation like rape. Whatever the reason, the decision to have a baby works from both sides of the third and fourth dimensions. During an abortion, the human is deciding that they are not ready, and the soul is retracting to incarnate at a later date. The future incarnation of that soul could be through the same mother or a different one. That soul may even choose to come down through the same genealogical line of the family by becoming a grandchild or great-grandchild.

There is no punishment for abortion. The physical body may be terminated, but the soul never dies. The soul is eternal and indestructible, retaining its own mind, personality and memory bank. The soul or souls you choose not to accept through birth are fine in the fourth dimension. This clarification should alleviate fear, guilt and blame for women who are in emotional agony over their decision to have an abortion.

Premature Death

When a child dies inexplicably from Sudden Infant Death Syndrome (SIDS), it is evidence that the soul has withdrawn its opportunity and has chosen to go back home to the spiritual worlds.

In Edgar Cayce's* readings for bereaved parents who had lost children, he never found fault or blamed anyone. He often said, "The soul has chosen to remain with its maker." On other occasions, Cayce told the parents, "The soul only needed to be near the parents for a short time for spiritual awakening." The spiritual awakening occurs when the parents, beset with grief, begin a spiritual search to understand the nature of life and death. After a time, this search leads them to people, groups and philosophies that help them understand that death is only an illusion. Edgar Cayce also said that when life in the physical plane is cut short—when a child dies young—that soul has experienced an eternity of love during the short hours, days or years lived on the earth. In a few brief moments of time, the baby experiences a lifetime of love.

There are no boundaries of time where love is concerned. When death comes to a child, it has indeed experienced all the love and light that can be experienced over a lifetime. The soul takes the precious love received during its short time on earth to the other side. There is no fault or blame; the soul simply changed its mind. In other cases, the soul departs early from the earthly life because it is needed for important work on the other side.

This spiritual perspective of miscarriage, stillborns, abortion and premature death should shed new light on the process of the soul's evolutionary journey. The above-referenced insights should help those who have experienced any of these situations to heal and move forward.

*Edgar Cayce is a well-known trance channel who was also called the "sleeping prophet." He conducted over fourteen thousand recorded readings in the early part of the twentieth century and passed away in 1945. Cayce founded the Association for Research and Enlightenment (ARE) in Virginia Beach, VA, where his vast library of readings are stored.

7 - *Prayer for Conception or Adoption of a Child*

There are many women who desperately want a child and haven't experienced a miscarriage, stillborn baby, abortion or SIDS. Many women are ready to have a child but have trouble conceiving. If a woman or couple is stressed or anxious, conception is highly unlikely to take place. Stress blocks the flow of procreation. If you have found that stress may be interfering with your fertility, consider taking a vacation near water. A healing and feminine element, water helps people to relax and go with the flow. You may also consider asking God for a specific soul to be your child. Before you go to sleep at night, say the following affirmation:

Dear Lord, please send a special soul to me from my soul group in heaven. I pray for a precious child to be conceived, to be born and to be healthy. I invite that soul into our lives now to fulfill the soul agreements that we have previously made. Thank you for hearing and answering my prayer.

Rest assured that if it is God's perfect will, there will soon be a pregnancy.

If you have relentlessly tried to no avail, open your heart to the possibility of adoption. Your baby will find you, even if it is through a surrogate route. There are no accidents with adoption, and so many precious babies need good homes. Couples who adopt could also conceive their own child shortly thereafter as the stress of getting pregnant finally subsides.

8 - Seeing Spirits in the Formative Years

During the ages of one to five, the soul is newly implanted in the physical body and is still connected to and able to communicate with other dimensions. Children of this delicate age can see, hear and feel their angels, guides and departed loved ones. Some children can see and talk about grandparents and great-grandparents from the other side who they've never met. Soul agreements made in the fourth dimension solidify who a child is surrounded by in the third dimension. For example, when a child says, "Grandpa was talking to me in my room last night," the parent should agree and ask, "What did your Grandpa look like? Did he tell you his name? What did he say or do?" Asking questions can also apply to children talking about invisible playmates, who can be other angels or guides. Sometimes babies will smile and coo while pointing up toward the ceiling; this could be because they are communicating with their angels or guides.

Once a child reaches the age of six or seven, they shut out the invisible realms because they enter a different energy frequency. This is a natural reaction, as it ensures a mode of self-preservation. Seeing the other side would be very distracting while at school or in a work situation. Forgetting about the spirit world is a form of protective amnesia. However, in some instances individuals retain the ability to see spirits and may even develop this ability further to become psychic mediums. Many of my clients excitedly share stories of their children's experiences and visions. At times, these youngsters even mention their past lives in detail. In an effort to dispel an overactive imagination, many parents seek out dates, times and facts from their children's stories and have their claims surprisingly validated.

I always encourage parents and grandparents of young children to keep a journal of the comments that are made. My own mother kept a journal, and I was amazed at what I said at age three: "I'm glad I picked you to be my mama!" "Don't you remember when I was here a long, long time ago?" And there were also stories about my invisible playmate, Pat. These were just a few of the insights that were recorded. These journals can make a wonderful keepsake for your child when they are older. Aside from being a sentimental gift, they can also provide great comfort to an older version of the soul that is seeking to find purpose and progression within this lifetime.

9 - Accidents, Murders, Suicides and Comas

Accidents
To many people, accidents are considered outside the realm of their control, an instance where fate steps in. But from a spiritual perspective, there are no accidents. Individuals who pass quickly in accidents have learned what they've needed to learn on the earth plane. The accidental event could also be a prearranged soul

agreement between parents and their child, a husband and wife, siblings and so on so that the family can learn emotional strength or faith by joining together.

It is not our place to ask why an accident happens. We should have the faith to know it's the soul's will and that the soul's purpose has been accomplished. There are many famous people throughout history who have been killed in car or plane accidents that have shocked the public. James Dean and Princess Diana quickly come to mind, but there are plenty more. And it's not just famous people; every second in this country, someone's relative or friend dies in some type of accident.

Souls that elect to undergo an accident as a form of exit from earth usually leave the body before the initial impact occurs. There is no pain or suffering, and the soul is greatly assisted by rescue angels and guides. Souls that choose to die quickly in accidents sometimes help others that pass in a similar manner. The help is instrumental in assisting these shocked souls in finding the light in the chaos of experiencing a new frequency. Often, when I'm doing a reading, a loved one who has passed in an accident will clap their hands to get my attention; they do so to let me know they passed quickly. They all tell me that they chose (at a soul level) to leave the way they did and are in the light and love of God.

It is important to pray for all souls who have crossed over. It doesn't matter in what manner they have made the transition. Remember, there is no prayer that goes unheard, and departed souls need our prayers for peace and progression.

Murders

I have received a lot of information from my angelic light beings on various subjects. They tell me that an intentional murder or a death in battle (which is similar to murder) is an agreement between souls to learn certain soul lessons. The individual that has been murdered has actually chosen to pass in that way. The perpetrator (during the life review) experiences not only the feelings of the victim, but also the emotions of those left behind. The murderer and victim meet again in the afterlife during the life review and discuss the emotions, hurt and the physical pain they endured. They also discuss what they learned from the experience. The process helps them gain additional soul knowledge. Spiritually, there are no victims in life; we choose everything at the soul level.

The motive behind a murder comes in many forms—anger, revenge, jealousy, insanity or necessity (as in a war situation or for self-defense). No soul is condemned by God; we only judge ourselves. There are karmic ties, but only if both souls choose and agree to carry out an action before they both are incarnated. A soul is never forced to rectify an action in a future lifetime. The murderer is held accountable for their actions and needs to address what has been done, heal from it and release that negative intent or action. They may choose to have their own life taken through murder in a future life to better understand this action, or they may choose to rectify their actions on the other side before being incarnated again.

Suicides

There has been a lot of controversy and many different opinions about the act of suicide. I have researched the subject and received information directly from my angels. First, there is no condemnation with suicide; we are all children of God and are unconditionally loved by Him. Suicide is merely a decision a person makes. Some engage in this act because of depression, some carry it out under the influence of alcohol or drugs, and others do it because the pressures of life became too overwhelming. The bottom line, though, is that there is no running away from self. We all need to evaluate and address our life after death to see if we have progressed.

Most people who commit suicide believe that their path is too difficult to endure. In the event of the intentional and premeditated suicide of a healthy person, the timeline for soul progression has been cut short. The soul agreement made with God and other souls has not been completed. In other words, if the soul makes an agreement before birth to pass away of natural causes at eighty but commits suicide at twenty, there are sixty years of experiences and soul lessons lost for growth and development in this lifetime. Just think of it as prerequisite course in high school or college that must be completed in order to graduate.

Of course, there are varying circumstances that surround suicide as well. September eleventh is a case in point. When people jumped from the trade tower windows out of panic to avoid death by fire, they were not committing a premeditated act. Another example that can be likened to the same idea is when someone jumps in front of a bullet to save another. There is a big difference between choosing to intentionally die and dying because of unforeseen circumstances. The person who tries to consciously run away from life commits a selfish act, not only for their own soul growth but also for the souls whom they made agreements with. This is especially true for those who are left behind, still suffering from the loss.

Many people who commit suicide go through a form of rehabilitation once they have passed. I have done readings in which souls who committed suicide come through, and every single one wishes they hadn't done it. However, there are angels and guides on the other side to help those souls adjust and move on. It may take several years (in earthly time) for them to acknowledge the act, forgive themselves and heal, but they always do.

Comas and Artificial Life Support

The soul goes in and out of the body when someone is in a coma. An invisible silver cord attached to the solar plexus keeps the body and soul connected. When we leave our bodies through astral travel in the sleep state, the cord stretches and the soul leaves through the top of the head to travel through the dimensions. Of course, if the cord snaps or breaks, we pass on. In a deep coma or vegetative state, the soul longs to make the transition but is still attached to the physical body. In some cases, the soul may stay out of the body permanently and watch what is happening in the room from an aerial view. When well-intending family members artificially keep someone alive, it is torturous for the one suffering in a coma. It is common for family members to try to keep their loved ones with them, even though it's best to release their soul. The soul chooses its own passing time. If the situation arises in your family, remember that everything is all a part of a bigger soul plan. You may be unknowingly imprisoning or holding your loved one's soul captive by keeping them alive.

10 - Animal Consciousness

In group sessions and one-on-one readings, sometimes a departed pet comes through to communicate. Animals have emotional feelings and a memory bank just like human beings do. They feel love, remorse, despair, joy and peace. When a human has a pet, such as a dog, cat or horse, and loves that animal dearly and unconditionally, a bond forms for all of eternity. If the pet's caretaker passes on first, the pet will feel loneliness and remorse. If the pet is carelessly given away or left behind, the animal will feel abandoned and sad. When mistreated, the pet will experience anxiety and physical pain. We need to be aware that all animals are sentient, feeling beings. They can also absorb negative energy from us to ease our emotional and physical discomfort.

Animals are highly intuitive and can see auras and spirits. Keep this in mind when your pet looks up and around in a room when no one else is there. Human souls cannot inhabit an animal body, for animals have their own unique mass consciousness. Think of each species as a sea of collective consciousness. Mammals are canine (dog or wolf), feline (cat), equine (horse), bovine (cow), to name a few. Avian is bird consciousness. Cold-blooded reptiles (snakes, lizards, etc.) make up another group of collective energy, as do sea mammals (dolphins and whales) and aquatic animals (fish). Then there are amphibians, which bridge the land and sea (turtles, frogs, etc.).

The point is once we love and befriend a particular animal, we personalize that small part of their mass consciousnesses. The energy of a pet and a human soul will bond and form soul groups in heaven. Our beloved pets wait for us if they pass away first. They can be incarnated with us in different lifetimes as well. Your domestic tabby cat may have been a lion with you in an African lifetime. Your pet dog may have been a wolf that you loved in a past Native American Indian lifetime. From my guides, I've received information that a feline will always be a feline energy. In other words, a cat won't become a horse or a lizard. Animals do not have human souls, so the energy or consciousness of that particular species enters the animal at birth. For example, when a dog passes on, its energy goes back to the mass consciousness of canine and regroups. If you acquire another puppy, the energy of the last pet dog can pull out of the canine consciousness and reenter your new puppy's body. It can also choose to stay in its canine collective and later pull out to be with you in a future lifetime. Again, it is unconditional love that binds human souls and animal consciousnesses together for eternity.

11 - *The Controversy of Homosexuality and Transgender (Sex Change)*

We are all co-creators with God, and because of free choice and free will, we are capable of choosing our own sex each lifetime. We can choose to be a boy or a girl before conception takes place or when our infant body is developing in the womb. The sex organs do not develop immediately, so there is time to change our minds and change our sex. We decide, along with help from our spirit guides, if it would be more advantageous to learn our soul lessons as a male or female. The course or destiny of a human life can change drastically when it is viewed from either a male or female perspective. The sex we choose also affects how we are treated in life. A female body gives one the ability to have children and softer personality traits. A male body displays physical strength and prowess and sometimes even the potential for higher-paying jobs. The dynamics in a family unit can drastically change and be affected by either sons or daughters. The soul must be objective in deciding if it wants to carry out its mission as a man or a woman.

One can decide on a certain sex at any point in the baby's development. And the soul can change its mind throughout that time. Hopefully, the decision happens before the sex organs are developed, but it could possibly occur afterwards. From a metaphysical viewpoint, this is when homosexuality occurs. Many homosexuals admit that they felt different from their own sex in early childhood. For example, a little girl may not want to wear dresses or bows in her hair. She may prefer playing with boys or engaging in masculine pursuits. This is how she feels deep inside, and it is quite different than being a mere tomboy. A boy may secretly want to wear dresses like his sisters or play with dolls instead of trucks. There are some individuals who claim they became homosexual from molestation or sexual abuse, and this may be true. For the most part, however, homosexuality has nothing to do with hormones or abuses but with the decision a soul made before birth—the choice to be a girl or boy—and the choice of sexual orientation.

Another issue that can overshadow this situation is one's past lives. For example, if a soul predominantly had past lives as a male and incarnates into a female body, there can be discomfort. The same applies vice versa. A soul can feel literally misplaced or imprisoned in a body that doesn't suit it. The decision to change sex can be an option for those who find it intolerable to live life with the body that they have.

It is important to balance both the feminine and masculine sides of one's nature. Everyone in the world, whether they are male or female, has a duality to their nature. The masculine side tends to be strong-willed, assertive, competitive, analytical and driven to succeed. On the other hand, the feminine side is more passive, creative, intuitive, nurturing and emotional. It's important in each lifetime to try to balance both sides for soul growth. Also remember that in the end, the loving creative force of the universe—God—isn't concerned about what sex you are during each lifetime. The only question asked at the end of each lifetime is, "How have you loved?" or, in essence, "What have you done from your heart for your fellow man and the planet?"

12 -*The Masculine and Feminine Elements of Nature*

Believe it or not, nature and the elements have a masculine and feminine essence. I am not referring to the actual reproduction systems used by plants but the essence they emit. Trees with fragrant needles, like pine, spruce or fir, are considered feminine. If you want to get in touch with your feminine side, stand beside a pine tree. It's very soothing. Flowering or fruit trees are also considered feminine, such as dogwood, cherry, apple or pear trees. Take a nature walk and try to be in the presence of trees with a feminine essence.

Trees that emanate power and strength are considered masculine—poplars, sycamores, mighty oaks, California redwoods and so on. If you want to enhance your masculine side, wrap your arms around the trunk of one of these majestic trees and give it a hug. Notice how grounded you feel doing it. If you are landscaping your property. It's a good idea to plant trees of both a masculine and feminine essence to incorporate balance around your home.

The four main elements—earth, air, fire and water—also have an essence. We have all heard the earth referred to as "Mother Earth," which personifies the feminine. The earth brings forth life and creates beauty. Water is a fluid, cleansing and healing element and also has a feminine essence. For example, apparitions of Mother Mary have occurred in the rain, and miraculous springs of water have appeared after her visitations. Father Sky, the element of air, has a masculine essence. Think of the force and power of tornadoes and hurricanes. Fire is considered masculine for heat, warmth and protection (not just for destruction). Air, the other masculine element, can "fan the flames" of fire and increase it, so they are compatible.

This knowledge will help you admire all of nature along with the elements that surround you. There is a distinct balance and harmony you can align yourself with in nature that can culminate into a calming and resounding peace in your life.

About the Author

Michele A. Livingston is an internationally known visionary, psychic medium and gifted artist. With a master's degree in art education, she taught art in public schools and later displayed her work in her own art gallery. Clairvoyant from an early age, she has the incredible ability to see and communicate with angels, departed loved ones and spirit guides.

In 1993, Mary, the Blessed Mother, appeared to Michele—which astounded the author because she was not raised Catholic. Mary entreated her to paint twelve different images of Mary's divine feminine energy. This event changed the author's life and is chronicled in her first book, *Visions from Mary*. A similar spiritual and artistic encounter with Red Cloud, the departed chief of the Lakota Sioux Indians, became the subject of her second book, *Echoes in the Wind*. Her third book, *Miraculous Encounters: True Stories of Experiences with Angels and Departed Loved Ones*, is a compilation of over one hundred inspirational stories of spiritual encounters by ordinary people. Her fourth book, *The True Nature of Love: Awakening to the Christ Consciousness,* contains inspirational prayers on a variety of subjects with a central theme, "love is the key to soul progression."

Michele has touched thousands of people—one-on-one and in seminars—with messages and actual visions of their departed loved ones. She has hosted her own radio talk show and has made numerous appearances on radio and TV. As a healer, counselor and ordained minister, she continues to bring messages and soul-healing stories to people all over the world and assists people in taking that "next step" in consciousness to become closer to the Creator.

Michele is available for radio and TV interviews, seminars, group sessions and phone and in-person consultations. For information please visit her website at: http://www.michelelivingston.com, or call (717) 737-3888.

Others books by Michele A. Livingston:

Visions from Mary

Miraculous Encounters:
   True Stories of Experiences with Angels
   and Departed Loved Ones

Echoes in the Wind:
   Messages from the Tribes of the Nation –
   Volume 1, The Lakota (Sioux) Nation

The True Nature of Love:
   Awakening to the Christ Consciousness

Available from the author at:
www.MicheleLivingston.com
or 717-737-3888